More praise for Al Gini's *The Importance of Being Lazy*

"Al Gini is to philosophy what Edison was to engineering—he subjects Great Ideas to the service of the common good. His reading of the human condition leads him to the conclusion that we need to take things a little more easy. Now I have powerful ammunition the next time someone wants me to get out of the hammock."

—Peter Sagal, Host of NPR's *Wait Wait . . . Don't Tell Me!*

"By degrees both scholarly and whimsical, and written by one of the hardest working people in leisure studies today . . . Al Gini delivers a brilliant narrative on the history of leisure as well as its ongoing necessity for workaholics today . . . This is an essential book."

—Daniel Born, editor of *The Common Review*, *The Great Books Foundation.*

"For all of us hyper-programmed, over-committed, Type-A workaholics, Al Gini has the prescription for what ails us: Put down the Palm Pilot and cancel the meeting. It's time to unplug, unwind, and rediscover the joy of play. God bless him."

—Steve Edwards, Host, *Eight-Forty Eight*, WBEZ-FM Chicago Public Radio

"This exquisitely researched offering provides sharp insight and a new perspective into why Americans must take vacations, why many feel they must escape if only for two weeks a year the ever-growing demands of what has become a pulverizing and dehumanizing daily grind"

—John Eckberg, career and workplace reporter for the *Cincinnati Enquirer*

"Gini is so persuasive I kept putting the book down to go out and play!"

—Eric Zorn, columnist for the *Chicago Tribune*

The Importance of Being Lazy

In Praise of Play, Leisure, and Vacations

The Importance of Being Lazy

In Praise of Play, Leisure, and Vacations

AL GINI

Routledge
New York and London

Published in 2003 by
Routledge
29 West 35th Street
New York, NY 10001
www.routledge-ny.com

Published in Great Britain by
Routledge
11 New Fetter Lane
London EC4P 4EE
www.routledge.co.uk

10 9 8 7 6 5 4 3 2 1

Cataloging-in-Publication Data is available from the Library of Congress

ISBN 0-415-93879-1 (hb)

To Mary Koenig, whose work put this book together.
To Damon Zucca, whose encouragement made this book possible.
To Sherry Gini, who makes life a pleasure and every
vacation an adventure!

If all the year were playing holidays,
To sport would be as tedious as to work;
But when they seldom come, they wished for come.

—William Shakespeare's Prince Hal, *King Henry IV, Part 1*

Contents

The Project and the Problem

More men are killed by overwork than the importance of the world justifies.

—Rudyard Kipling

The history of labor and work is long and convoluted. The history of not working is short. Paid downtime, vacations, leisure are, for the vast majority of working folks, perks of the postindustrial age. Clearly, Melville's whalers, Dickens's sweatshop workers, and Sinclair's meatpackers knew nothing of holidays, sick time, and personal days off.

What many of us now take to be a standard part of the annual rights of summer—time off, travel, organized play—was, until recently, the exclusive preserve of the aristocracy, the landed gentry, and the nouveau rich. It is only since World War II that the general American workforce has taken to the roads with a vengeance, spent quality time with the kids in a cabin in Connecticut, or traveled to Europe and beyond. And it is only since the success of Disneyland that the travel industry has committed itself to the goal of offering every man, woman, and child in America the opportunity to spend two weeks on the "Love Boat Cruise" of their choice.

My thesis is a simple one. Even if we love our jobs and find creativity, success, and pleasure in our work, we also crave, desire, and need not to work. No matter what we do to earn a living, we all seek the benefits of leisure, lassitude, and inertia. We all need to play more in our lives.

As a nation, by living out the virtues of our Puritan past and pioneering forefathers, we have achieved unparalleled success. In being "dutiful soldiers" and "diligent in our toil," we have created a land of riches and opportunity. Of course, there are some real downsides connected to our collective efforts and achievements.

Like it or not, too many of us, out of desire or necessity, choice or chance, put too much time in on the job. We have made a fetish out of work. It's now part of our character and culture. We have become addicted to the *promise* of work. Work *promises* we will get ahead. Work *promises* power, money, and influence. Work *promises* we will be accepted, respected, successful. And so, we work. We work because we want to, because we need to. We work out of habit and desire. We work to occupy time. We work to establish our place in the pecking order, to guarantee status and prestige. And, too often, we work because we simply don't know what else to do with ourselves, because we think we must and should.

But even if we don't overwork, even if we are not certifiable workaholics, work still preoccupies our lives. Most of us will spend the majority of our adult conscious life on the job. It has simply become standard to respond to the conventional salutation of "Hello, how are you?" with some version of the refrain "*I am so busy!*" Unfortunately, we say this to one another with no small degree of pride, as if our exhaustion were a trophy and our ability to keep going a mark of real character. As theologian Wayne Muller has pointed out: "The busier we are, the more important we seem to ourselves and, we imagine, to others." Sadly, to be busy, to be unavailable, has become the model of the successful life.[1]

Although we use being busy as our mantra and our model, there is some research suggesting that even though we claim to adhere to the strict interpretation of the Protestant work ethic, most of us in fact really don't "walk the talk" or put in as much time on the job as conventional wisdom would lead us to believe. In a 1997 study titled *Time for Life: The Surprising Ways Americans Use Their Time*, the time use experts John Robinson and Geoffrey Godbey of Penn State University argue that despite all the intrusions and demands upon people's lives these days, Americans in the 1990s have more leisure than ever before. Not everyone of course. A working single mother of two children doesn't have as much time as a sixty-five-year-old empty nester. And, of course, a married father of four isn't as carefree as a twenty-year-old single male. But in general, say the authors, Americans are working less than they did thirty years ago— about fifty hours per week, which includes paid work time, household chores, and commuting. And Americans, say the authors, now enjoy close to forty hours of leisure per week, five more hours than we had in 1965. "People think they are work- ing longer hours," says Godbey, "but in reality, they mistake the pace of work for length of time spent working. On average, the number of hours people spend working has diminished."[2]

Needless to say, this is a controversial thesis and one that has received a lot of criticism because it seems to directly counter the pace and feel of our lives. The authors, however, aren't sur- prised by this reaction. The problem, they claim, is that the soci- ety we live in values and measures time—"being busy has become a status symbol." We constantly brag about being busy, say the authors of the report, because being busy means we are important. Hence, when people are asked how many hours they work, eat, tend to children, do chores, and so on, they exagger- ate. So instead of just asking them, Robinson and Godbey required their ten thousand survey participants to keep a minute-by-minute, 24-hour diary of how they spent their days. The results were surprising. When asked, women claimed that they put in 40.4 hours per week on the job, and men claimed they put in 46.2 hours. When calculated from diary entries, women actually put in 32 hours per week and men worked 40.4 hours per week.[3]

Robinson and Godbey's research wants to change the agreed-upon number of hours we claim to be on the job. I think their numbers are wrong. I think they are way too conservative. But no matter the exact numbers, it doesn't change how this society sees itself and deals with the issues of work, time, and self-importance. Although it may well be true that people mistake working faster and being more rushed with working longer, Robinson and Godbey's data also indicate and reinforce the overall thesis that busyness, constant rushing, and stress are huge problems in our society. Numbers aside, the point is that the feeling of being pushed, overworked, or too busy is primarily about attitude, concentration, and orientation, and not just about the actual hours we put in on the job. There may be lots of debate about how much time Americans spend working, but there's no disputing that it "feels" like we're working more. When it comes to feeling busy—no matter what they told you in logic class—perception is reality!

Of course, just because we put in so many hours on the job doesn't mean we like it. But love it or hate it, work sets the pace and establishes the rhythm for everything else we do in life. Alexis de Tocqueville may have been the first to recognize and report on the energy and busyness of Americans, both in their work and in their private lives, but he was by no means the last. James Gleick, in *Faster: The Acceleration of Just About Everything*, reflects on why Americans (and, increasingly, the world) work and play as hard and intensely as they do. Gleick suggests that we have always been time and task obsessed, but now due to the "rapid heartbeat of technology" we can squeeze more and more of everything into the allotted time span. We are now manic about speed, says Gleick. The world now seems to operate on five-minute intervals. We are rush freaks. We are time obsessed.

"Lose not a minute" is the motto of the age. We are always making haste. Multitasking isn't an option, it's a way of life. Hyperactivity is the norm. As Gleick sees it:

> We humans have chosen speed and we thrive on it—more than we generally admit. Our ability to work fast and play fast gives us power. It thrills us. If we have learned the name of just one hormone, it is adrenaline. No wonder we call sudden exhilaration a rush. "Your life is lived with the kind of excitement that your forbearers knew only in battle," observes the writer Mark Helprin. And: "They unlike you, were the prisoner of mundane tasks. They wrote with pens, they did addition, they waited endlessly for things that come to you instantaneously, they had far less than you do, and they bowed to necessity, as you do not. You love the pace, the giddy, continual acceleration." Admit it—you do![4]

Here's the problem. When life becomes an Olympic endurance event ("the Everydayathon"), when the stopwatch is always ticking, when are we supposed to have fun? When will there be a time to be human?[5] As Benjamin Kline Hunnicutt, professor of leisure studies, so aptly put it, "Having to go so fast to keep up, we miss stuff—our existence is truncated. Some things simply cannot be done going full speed: love, sex, conversation, food, family, friends, nature. In the whirl, we are less capable of appreciation, enjoyment, sustained concentration, sorrow, memory."[6]

I think, if we can be honest with ourselves, we all do too much or try to do too much. My mother used to accuse me of having "eyes bigger than your stomach." She told me that I both literally and figuratively put too many things on my plate. "Alfredó," she'd say, "You do too much. Slow down, take smaller bites, or you're not going to enjoy anything. "Piano, piano arrive sano!" (Slowly, slowly, and you'll get there surely, safely!)

Even when we're not at work, when we're not on the clock,

we consume time by constantly doing things and staying busy. Weekends are whirlwinds of activity. Vacations often resemble a blitzkrieg of organized movement with every moment of the trip preplanned and orchestrated for maximum efficiency and, of course, pleasure! For example—"Twenty-one countries in 14 days: Airfare, ground transportation, guides, lodging, meals, wine but not cocktails, and all tips included!"—perfect, don't you think? At the risk of sounding like a Jean-Paul Sartre wanna-be: "We just don't do no-thing well!"

Here's a series of statistics I think more accurately reflects how long we work and how we spend our time. According to the *Harvard Health Letter*, leisure time has dramatically eroded in recent decades, down to approximately 16.5 hours, per person, per week. The Bureau of Labor Statistics claims that dual-income married couples are now the most common type of household unit in America, numbering 31 million, or 39 percent of all working households. On average, these married couples work 26 percent longer each year than similar married couples did 30 years ago.[7] In the 1950s, commentators worried about how we would all use the extra unstructured leisure time that was being generated by the "automation revolution." Ha! Instead of free time, we ended up with a national epidemic of overwork, stress, and too little time for work or rest. A recent surgeon general's report declared that the lack of "leisure-time physical activity" has become a serious health threat. About one in four American adults reports not having time to participate in any form of physical activity.[8] Finally, besides more of us working more hours per week than ever before, more of us are working more weeks a year than ever before. According to a report issued by the United Nations, U.S. workers average 49.5 weeks of work each year.[9]

Joe Robinson, former editor of the travel magazine *Escape*, used to make a living by going on vacation. Robinson claims that "we're the most vacation-starved country in the industrial world!" In this society, says Robinson, we perversely allow "downtime for machinery for maintenance and repair, but we don't allow it for the employees." America's most hazardous work-related illness, says Robinson, is "vacation deficit disorder" or "vacation starvation." Robinson believes that every American should, by federal law, be guaranteed a minimum three-week vacation per year with pay, increasing to four weeks after three years. For Robinson, life is too short—so, "work to live" don't "live to work." "Workers and travelers of America, unite! We have nothing to lose but our stress!"[10]

Robinson and the surgeon general are not alone in their warnings regarding the lack of leisure and vacation time and potential health issues. A fourteen-year study of 12,866 men published in The Journal of Psychosomatic Medicine found that annual vacations sharply reduced the risk of death in middle-aged men. Similarly, a twenty-year study of 749 middle-aged women by the Centers for Disease Control found a direct link between a lack of vacations and a higher risk of heart attack and death. At the University of Essex, England, researchers found a link in women between working more than forty-eight hours a week for more than three years and high blood pressure, as well as ailments of the arms, legs, and hands. Finally, the National Institute for Occupational Safety and Health claims that demanding jobs that give employees little control over their work increase the risk of heart disease. Conclusion: "Vacations may be good for your health."[11]

Unfortunately, too many Americans, primarily men, but increasing numbers of women too, only alter their patterns, habits, and lifestyles when they absolutely have to. On more than one occasion, I've bumped into a male friend I haven't seen in years who has lost weight, is sporting a fresh tan, and is looking great. Almost invariably his response to my question "What's new?" is some version of "I had a heart attack, a stroke, cancer surgery, or_____[fill in the blank]. It made me think. It made me see the handwriting on the wall. It made me change." On many more occasions, however, I'll bump into a widow of an old friend who will relate a similar scenario, but with a much less happy outcome. Sadly, sometimes we give ourselves permission to change only when we're confronted by a crisis that we can use as an excuse.

In a cover story in the *Utne Reader*, Mark Harris argues that most children don't live their lives by a day planner, Palm Pilot, or a Rolodex. Kids live life in the moment. They use their imagination to seek out adventure, silliness, and laughter at every opportunity. A child's world, says Harris, despite parental rules and regulations, is simmering with fun. Children, says Harris, are masters of play. They need to play. It's what they do. It's the way they ingest the world. It's the way they learn. By acting out or playing out a situation they acquire cognitive and motor skills. In play, they create a map of reality and come to know and define the other players in the game. Play, says the psychiatrist Lenore Terr, is not frivolous. It is one of the ways we become human. Play, like laughter, says Terr, is crucial at every stage of life. Play, for both children and adults alike, helps us unlock the door to the world and ourselves. Sadly, Terr concludes, the rush of modern life means less spontaneity, more scheduling, and the slow erosion of the time and opportunity to play.[12]

All of us need to play more. All of us need to "vacate" ourselves from our jobs and the wear and tear of the "everyday-ness" of our lives. All of us need to get absorbed in, focused on, something of interest outside of ourselves. All of us need escape, if only for a while, to retain our perspective on *who we are* and *who we don't want to be*. All of us need to gain some feeling for, some knowledge of, the differences between distraction and insight, merriment and meaning, entertainment and recreation, laziness and leisure, rest and inertia.

The ability to play, to go on vacation, to take long walks, to have a quiet weekend, to have time to think, should not be perceived as a perk or privilege. We need not always be doing. In fact, we must all try to *studiously do less*, in order *to be more*.

If we are what we do, then to a great extent, as adults, we are defined by *our work and our play*. Both of these basic patterns of behavior influence not only how we define ourselves but how we understand and interpret reality and how we make ethical choices about our lives and our interactions with others. Therefore, depending upon who we want to be, and how we want to be known, we must be very careful in our choices of what we do for a living and how we choose to play. Remember, to borrow a couple of rather classic phrases, "leisure can be the basis of culture," the "enzyme of a quality life," or it can simply be "the catalyst for camp and kitsch."

This book is a brief breakdown of what we do when we are not on the job. It's a look at how we rest, recreate, and play. It's a window into why we venerate vacation time, how we spend our time and money when not on the job, and why we all work so very hard at trying to have fun. This slim text does not attempt to cover every conceivable vacation option from Alaska to Zimbabwe. As the Chicago radio mogul Pat Fitzpatrick said to me, "Whatever you do keep it short! Who's got time to read a lot of stuff about leisure?" Nor does it attempt to address all the possible definitions, differences and nuances regarding the terms *recreation*, and *re-creation*, *leisure*, *play*, *jobs*, and *work*. (According to Wayne Booth, scholar and bibliophile, such an endeavor would require a lifetime. The University of Chicago library alone contains 32 books on recreation and re-creation, 119 books on leisure, 150 books on play, and literally thousands of books on the various aspects of work, jobs, and careers in our lives.[13])

This book is a highly eclectic, idiosyncratic, and hopefully philosophical survey of how we play and why we need leisure in our lives. I believe that Thomas Carlyle was wrong, or at the very least exaggerating, when he said: "Work is the grand cure of *all of the maladies and miseries* that ever beset mankind" (italics mine). I believe that the purpose of life is probably closer to pleasure and play than it is to simple drudgery and toil. Unfortunately, I also believe, too many of us confuse leisure and play with mindless distractions, excessive consumerism, and do-nothing laziness.

Having said all of this, let me warn those readers who are looking for a single theory or formula by which to achieve leisure in their lives that they will be disappointed in what follows. Yes, there is some theory involved in the pursuit of leisure. Yes, there is some study and preparation required to achieve leisure. But, in the end, we learn leisure by living it. It's about giving ourselves over to it. It's an art form that we have to directly experience. Perhaps the late great violinist Isaac Stern ironically and indirectly makes the point about how we achieve leisure in his comment about how we *don't come* to appreciate music: "Learning music by (simply) reading about it is like making love by mail."

In the immediate aftermath of 9-11-01 both the national psyche and the economy went into shock if not complete paralysis. Within three weeks two national airlines declared bankruptcy and literally closed their hanger doors. Within a month, a reputed 110,000 airline workers were laid off or furloughed indefinitely and 20 percent of all flight schedules were canceled. According to the Bureau of Labor Statistics, the economy lost 480,000 jobs in October 2001 and another 331,000 jobs in November, thereby bringing the national unemployment rate to 5.7 percent, its highest level since August 1995.[14] Moreover, retail sales dropped 2.4 percent in September, rallied in October by 6.4 percent, plunged again in November by 3.7 percent, and stayed steady but were not sensational during the December Christmas rush.[15]

Besides its immediate impact on the airlines, 9-11-01, not so surprisingly, had a devastating impact on the vacation, restaurant, and hospitality industries. For example, Disney World and Disneyland stayed open and soldiered on, but in the immediate aftermath of 9-11-01, cancellation rates exceeded 60 percent. In the months that followed, although attendance did pick up, both of the Magic Kingdoms could be best typified as "ghost towns." Hardest hit was Disney World in Orlando, Florida, which sharply reduced the schedules for all of its 40,000 hourly workers, and asked its 7,400 salaried employees to voluntarily cut their paychecks and workweeks to thirty-two hours. Regionally, economists claimed that in excess of 60,000 waiters, waitresses, fast-food workers, restaurant cooks, hotel housekeepers, and the like either lost their jobs or had their hours reduced due to the decline in tourism after 9-11-01.[16]

At "ground zero," Mayor Rudolph Guiliani—the unexpected Churchill to arise out of the ashes of the Twin Towers and *Time* magazine's Man of the Year—was in front of the media, seemingly every hour on the hour, for weeks giving status reports, keeping the nation informed, offering prayers, offering advice, flying the flag, rallying the troops, and acting as a "cheerleader" and "Big-Apple Booster." He implored us: "Don't let them win!" "Show them our spirit!" "Show them what Americans are made of!" "Let's live our lives!" "Come to New York!" "See a play!" "Go shopping!" "Go out to dinner!" "Let's get back to normal again!"

We will, of course, recover. But I wonder if we'll ever be *normal* again, or if we ever want to be *normal* again? As Sue Shellenbarger of the *Wall Street Journal* so eloquently put it, "Across the nation, at nearly every level of the workforce, a subtle, but far-reaching shift in priorities is underway. Values that were pre-eminent for many people—career, status, money, personal fulfillment—now are taking a back seat to more fundamental human needs: family, friends, community, connectedness with others."[17]

I think that life-changing events can spark serious changes in our priorities. It doesn't mean, however, that we're going to reprioritize everything instantly. But, at the very least, I think it forces us to pause and reflect on things we take for granted: the role of work in our lives; being preoccupied by the pursuit of status, stuff, and success; how, when, and where we spend time with our families; and the quality of our friendships and relationships with others.

In a very basic sense, I think 9-11-01 is going to force us to reexamine our priorities on and off the job in regard to how we work and how we play. It is my hope that we will learn or relearn two complementary and fundamental truths regarding the human situation. (1) Adults *need* work in the same way that children *need* play in order to fulfill themselves as persons. (2) Adults need *play* in the same way that children need *play* in order to fulfill themselves as persons.

> [A]n overworked man is an unimaginative one, at best dully completing a routine, at worst making serious mistakes. Far from benefiting his company, he is very likely creating problems rather than solving them—and so making work for other overworked men to boast about. We get new ideas when our mind is allowed to roam in a free and relaxed way around a problem—and for that we need a reasonable amount of leisure and thus a decent annual vacation.
>
> Maybe the European practice of five weeks paid vacation goes too far—but not by much! (John Sullivan, columnist, *Chicago Sun-Times*, January 1, 2002)

one

The Other Side of Leisure
WORK, DAMN IT!

I do not like work even when someone else does it.

—Mark Twain

Aristotle said, "We work in order to have leisure." Who of us can seriously disagree with this statement? Another line from Aristotle, "we are unleisurely in order to achieve leisure" Could anything be clearer? And yet according to the statistics generated by the Department of Labor, as adults there is nothing we do more with our lives than work. From approximately the ages of 21 to 70, we will spend our lives working. We will not sleep as much, spend as much time with our families, eat as much, or recreate and rest as much as we will work. Whether we love our work or hate it, succeed in it or fail, achieve fame or infamy through it, we are all, like Sisyphus, condemned to push and chase that thing we call our job, our career, our work all of our days. "Even those of us who desperately don't want to work," said Ogden Nash, "must work in order to earn enough money so that they won't have to work anymore!" Like it or not, our collective leitmotif is not leisure but labor!

America has always been a land and a society of contrasts and paradoxes. One of the most glaring conflicts in our constellation of cultural values is our duplicitous attitude in regard to the Protestant work ethic. On the one hand, we have always praised work. We have cultivated an almost mystical reverence in its regard. We have preached that all honest work is character building and the means by which individuals achieve identity, integrity, and admission into the "club of adulthood." To deliberately choose not to work, not to have a job when work is available, is to be a social outcast. Worse yet, it means your mother now has the right to call you a bum!

On the other hand, let's be frank, we also think that work stinks! We just don't say it out loud all that often. Although work preoccupies our adult lives, most of us don't want it to. Few of us eagerly seek it out. Fewer still happily embrace its burdens and demands. And given the option, a lot of us would gladly never work again.

When you think about it, the only people who praise work are historians, politicians, or business owners who have to because it's in their best interest—it's their job! (Oh sure, you'll find the likes of Wendell Berry, farmer, poet, and essayist, praising—at least in public prose—the virtue of drudgery. But believe me, he's the exception to the rule, and, again, it's his job!) Studs Terkel is right. Don't ask bosses about work. What do you expect them to say? Of course, they're going to be for it. If you really want to know what people think of work, talk to workers. Chances are, says Terkel, they'll tell you stuff that would make Benjamin Franklin, Martin Luther, and John Calvin shake their heads in disbelief and blush with embarrassment.

American popular culture, says Julia Keller, *Chicago Tribune* columnist, is a much more accurate barometer of what people think about work than an academic survey or an uplifting op-ed piece written for Labor Day. The unruly truth that lies beneath the surface of our national commitment to the sacred icon of the Protestant work ethic, says Keller, is that "work is for saps" and should be avoided whenever possible. [1]

A lot of us may have nightmares about the job, but what

most of us fantasize about is—not working! We dream about having unlimited leisure. We imagine lives that are idle, lax, lazy, and, of course, rich too! We yearn for an existence that is exclusively directed at "working at play" and having fun. For most of us, work is a means to an end: status, stuff, cash, and lots of time off. We put up with it because we have to, but in our heart of hearts, many of us secretly wish we had been born into the J. Paul Getty or Bill Gates families. And even more of us are in complete agreement with yet another icon of American culture, Abraham Lincoln.

> My father taught me to work, but not to love it. I never did like to work, and I don't deny it. I'd rather read, tell stories, crack jokes, talk, laugh—anything but work.[2]

The philosopher Josef Pieper said that "we are fettered to the process of work."[3] Translation: We are captives of our jobs; we are consumed and time bound by what we do. Well, you don't have to be a scholar or a sage to know, or at least feel, that Pieper is right. Our lives do seem busier, fuller, more fatiguing than ever before. The sociologist Arlie Russell Hochschild suggests that modern workers talk about sleep in the same way that hungry people talk about food.[4]

A lot of us know all too well that we put a lot of time in on the job, and there is a raft of statistical sources that reinforces this feeling. The economist Juliet Schor estimates that annual hours on the job, across all industries and occupations, have been increasing over the last twenty years, so that the average employee is now on the job an additional 163 hours, or the equivalent of an extra month per year. In her 1991 best-seller, *The Overworked American*, she claimed that one-fourth of all full-time workers spent 49 or more hours on the job each week. Of these, almost half were at work 60 hours or more.[5] The management guru Charles Hardy noted in 1994 that the typical American worked 47 hours per week, for an annual total of 2,330 hours, and that in 2014 the average American worker would put in 3,000 hours per year on the job.[6] In 1996, Thomas Geoghegan, labor lawyer and syndicated columnist, estimated that middle-management types and senior executives endure a 55-to-65-hour week, and that 11 percent of all workers report working more than 65 hours per week.[7] In 1997, in her important analysis on work and the family, *The Time Bind*, Arlie Russell Hochschild reported that both men and women workers average slightly more than 47 hours a week.[8] Finally, in a 1999 study, a Cornell University research project found that, on average, Americans work 350 hours more per year than Europeans—and 70 hours more a year than even the Japanese, whose language contains the word *karoshi*, which means "death from overwork."[9] If some of these figures and projections are accurate, by the year 2010, the average workweek could exceed 58 hours.

What has to be kept in mind, of course, is that these figures reflect only hours on the job and do not represent the other aspects of our workday such as getting to and from the job as well as household and family responsibilities. A 1993 survey conducted by the Families and Work Institute of New York concluded that both spouses in a double-income household with kids put in a minimum of fifteen hours a day on work, commuting, chores and children.[10] These figures, based on a Monday-through-Friday schedule, mean that both spouses have already "logged in" seventy-five hours before the weekend. Moreover, although Sundays in many households are still reserved for family outings and social events, Saturdays are usually just another workday. "Honey-do lists" are drawn up, chores are assigned, projects are attended to, and kids are schlepped to music lessons and the mall.

Whatever the exact amount of time each of us is putting into the job, it is both palpably and statistically clear to most of us that we are working harder and longer than ever before. And more than just the extra time we are putting in on the job, the tempo, intensity, and stresses associated with our work seem to

"Great News" by Horsey. © 2001 Seattle Post-Intelligencer Tribune Media Services. Used with permission.

be accelerating. We cram more and more into each day, and yet we feel that we never have enough time to do all that must be done. In a 2001 phone survey of over a thousand households, the Families and Work Institute discovered that American families feel overworked and that they are doing too much on the job. Of those surveyed 55 percent reported feeling overwhelmed by how much work they have to do; 45 percent felt that they have to do many jobs at once and multitask too often; 59 percent complained that they were unable to reflect on and perfect the work they were doing; and, finally, 90 percent agreed strongly that they work "too fast" and "too hard" and they "never have enough time to get a job done properly."[11]

Some scholars of American culture claim that we are a nation "predisposed to hard work," that the "elevation of work over leisure" is an ethos that has long permeated our lives, and that we have made a religion out of our commitment to work. My question is: Who have these scholars been talking to? I'm sure that's exactly the kind of puritanical response you'd expect to get from Cotton Mather or from the nineteenth-century industrialist John D. Rockefeller, or perhaps find in the pseudopsychological scribblings of Frederick Winslow Taylor. But it's certainly not the kind of comment most workers would come up with.

Oh sure, there are people who really love their jobs, people for whom the line between work and play has vanished, people who find meaning and purpose in what they do. People who eagerly seek out their jobs, everyday. But let's not kid ourselves—these happy few represent a minority of the workforce!

For most of us—white collar or blue, good job or bad, decent pay or not—work is a chore, a task, a responsibility, a duty, something we are required to do to earn a living or maintain a lifestyle. Work for too many of us is perceived as "downtime," "dead time"—something that must be done, but there's little or no fun to be had in doing it. Most of us endure our jobs and put up with them because we have to, because we want to get paid. Perhaps the late *Chicago Tribune* columnist Mike Royko comes closest to the spirit of the "common man's" feeling about work when his alter ego in the column, Slats, says:

> [W]hy do we think the lottery is so popular? Do you think anybody would play if the super payoff was a job on the night shift in a meat packing plant? People play it so if they win they can be rich and idle . . . like I told you years ago—if work is so good, how come they have to pay us to do it?[12]

During the Viagra economy of the Clinton administration, the unemployment rate hit an unprecedented low of 3.9 percent. Perhaps for the first time ever, employees in every skill set were in demand, and employers from McDonald's to Microsoft were vigorously pursuing them with offers of high wages and big benefits. Employees, at least for a short time, were in the driver's seat and they knew it. They wanted to be courted. They wanted to be wooed. They wanted benefits and perks, and next to more money and meaningful work, they wanted time off.

According to a Families and Work Institute 1999 study, 63 percent of Americans say they want to work less, up from only 17 percent in 1994. In another 1999 study conducted by New York University and the University of Pennsylvania it was found that "45 to 50 percent of workers (and 80 percent of those working more than 50 hours a week) said they would prefer to work fewer hours, and more than 25 percent said they would take a pay cut to make it happen." Another survey in 2000 found that even college students and recent graduates place "flexible hours" at the top of the list of the job benefits they most desire—above health insurance, vacations, and stock options.[13] The moral of all this seems clear. Workers are united in their belief that even a good job, a great job, a job with terrific pay, perks, and prestige can demand too much of us. Jobs can eat up too much of our time, our energy, our passion, and our inner selves.

When Merle Haggard bellowed the lyrics "Take this job and shove it!" and Dolly Parton belted out "Nine to Five," both were voicing the frustrations of millions of us. Bad jobs suck! Even good jobs can be overrated! In fact, no job would be ideal! To quote poetry rather than country and western music, in the words of Philip Larkin (former poet laureate of England and *definitely not a saloon singer*):

> Why should I let the toad work
> Squat on my life?
> Can't I use my wit as a pitch fork
> And drive the brute off?[14]

The double irony in all of this is, of course, that although survey after survey reports that we do not like our jobs and that most of us would prefer not to work as much as we do, statistics suggest that given the raw hours we put in on the job, we are fast becoming a nation of workaholics. Former Secretary of Labor Robert Reich, in his book *The Future of Success*, says that the causes of our workaholism are both immediate and international: our consumer culture, advances in technology, increased competition, and the global marketplace. He is, of course, undoubtedly right. But I also think that the root cause of our workaholism is connected in large part to who we are as a nation and as a people.

As a society, we are obsessed with time. We have always been so; it's part of our national character. In this society, time is money and we always try to spend it well. We fail to understand and often scoff at the tradition of the siesta in Italy, Spain, and Mexico. We smirk at the French practice of closing down in August and Sweden's mandated five-week minimum vacation policy. We have never been comfortable with the abstract notion of free time. It is not in our nature to just let time pass. Unstructured time, dead time, downtime, wasted time—makes us ill at ease.

We see time as our most precious commodity. We try to make the most of our time. We fill time, use time, invest and manage time. We strive to be productive with our time. We live by schedules and lists. We micromanage all of our worktime, much of our playtime, and, increasingly, more and more of our family/private time. We have embraced Thomas Alva Edison's admonition that success is dependent upon "one-percent inspiration and ninety-nine percent perspiration." We pursue success by pouring our sweat and our energy into time. We believe that successful people always have time to do something more, and unsuccessful people never have enough time to do what must be done.

Although perception does not always equal reality, our perception that time must be used wisely and well does, in fact, constitute how we view reality. We have equated time with productivity and success. We desire time, covet time, and our greatest fear is the loss of time. We are in a constant race with and against time.

Historically, Americans have always viewed the active life as morally superior.[15] The tradition of "busyness" is part of our moral fabric; we accord kudos to those individuals who make every moment count and whose every movement is regulated by the clock. Traditionally, in this society, we measure meaning by productivity. And our obsession with time has always been directly connected to our addiction to work. The University of Iowa historian Benjamin K. Hunnicutt has suggested that whether by choice or circumstances, we have always lived in "a culture of work."[16] As a people, we have always been compulsive about what we do and how we do it. How else can we explain this nation's accomplishments in such a relatively short period of time? The nineteenth-century union demand for a limited workday was not about our unwillingness to work. It was about our unwillingness to work long hours for bad pay, in horrible conditions, and without the realistic possibility of improving our lot in terms of cash, possessions, and class.

In a quintessential American way being busy, being overworked conveys status and self-worth.[17] The busier our schedules, the more important we feel and the more we are able to acquire the possessions and things that supposedly constitute the good life. The lesson we learned as a nation from the Depression is that no matter what abuses can occur, no matter how vulnerable the individual worker can be, no matter what the threats to the human and civil rights of workers, "there is nothing better than work."[18] After we had endured the stark reality of no work and doing without for too long, all work, any work seemed preferable. We have learned too well that without work, time is unstructured, unproductive, and lacking in both purpose and profit. As a nation, we came out of the deprivations of the Depression and the rationed priorities of World War II seeking not to escape from or transcend work but rather to find transcendence through our work.

In this society, workaholism is considered to be a clean addiction, and one prized by businesses and corporations. After all, what company wouldn't rather have a workaholic instead of an alcoholic employee? Workaholics produce worth, make money, achieve success. Workaholism is one of the only addictions that is not merely condoned but actually rewarded. It is socially accepted and promoted because it is socially productive. We all know people who brag about working sixty, seventy, or even eighty hours per week.[19] Workaholics in effect say: "I know I'm a workaholic, but it's better than a lot of other things I could be! I'm not sailing a yacht. I'm not playing all day long. I'm not taking exotic trips. I'm working my damn ass off!" They assume, as do their families, friends, and colleagues, that they are being dutiful, industrious, and on the fast track to success as it's prescribed in the American Dream.

According to Diane Fassel in her important but underappreciated book, *Working Ourselves to Death*, the American/Protestant work ethic and workaholism are two separate and distinct phenomena. The work ethic is about the role and acceptance of work in our lives. It's about God's calling to work, the dignity and duty of work, the value and purpose of work. It's about personal and communal fulfillment and survival through work. The work ethic is about life and living. Workaholism, says Fassel, is just the opposite. Workaholism is a substitute for life. It's about self-absorbed, compulsive behavior and performance fixation. Workaholism is about addiction.

As an addiction, work becomes a narcotic: our surrogate, our palliative, our coping mechanism for life. Workaholism insulates and isolates us from life. It is an opiate that buffers us from ourselves and others. Workaholism is one way of dealing with reality when other options are unavailable. Work addiction may not be our first or best option, but it is a familiar and well-sanctioned one. "Workaholics," says Fassel, "are no longer 'showing up' for life. They are alienated from their own bodies, from their own feelings, from their own creativity, and from family and friends. They have been taken over by the compulsion to work and are slaves to it. They no longer own their lives."[20] Workaholism, she warns, is a progressively fatal disease, "which masquerades as a positive trait (or at least, an acceptable vice) in the cultural lore of our nation."[21]

Moreover, says Fassel, workaholics are not just job addicts. The addiction does not stop at the front door. It comes with you wherever you go. The workaholic lacks boundaries; the work process provides everything. Workaholics take work to bed, take it home on weekends, take it on vacation. The workaholic is never without work, because work is the fix. Many children of workaholic parents, Fassel said, describe vacations as whirlwinds of exhausting activity. Their parents did vacations the way they did work—full tilt and nonstop.[22]

In its narrowest sense, argues Fassel, workaholism is an addiction to action. The type of action may vary, but the process is the same: you leave yourself by losing yourself in your action/work.[23] Workaholics cannot say no to work and its demands. As addicts, they are driven by the compulsion to work. Work orientates them, affirms them, comforts them, holds out to them the possibility of happiness. Of course, says Fassel, for the true addict, the work is never done. Thus happiness dangles like the proverbial carrot: it's always the next project away.[24] Then they will have succeeded; then they will be happy; then they will be able to provide for all of their family's wants and needs.

Unfortunately, says Fassel, what compounds the problem for the workaholic is a social and business structure that actively rewards work addiction. We are a nation of addicted workers primarily because we are a nation of addictive work organizations. In an addictive society, says Fassel, workaholism does not shock us: there is no dissonance in this disease; it feels normal because it is the norm. We are used to it because it is part of what we are used to. Workaholism is the status quo. We have created a series of positive myths about workaholism: "No one ever died of hard work." "Workaholism is always profitable for individuals and corporations." "Workaholics always get ahead." "Hard work keeps you out of trouble." "No effort goes unrewarded." "Success comes to those who work for it." "Work proves worth." "Fitness addicts have good bodies; workaholics make more money." "Having it all is not an illusion." "The only line is the bottom line." "Business is war; to the victors go the spoils." Homilies such as these comfort and numb us. We have adapted to workaholism, says Fassel, in much the same way a frog can adapt to a pot of boiling water. If you suddenly drop a frog into boiling water it will leap out immediately. But, says Fassel, if you put a frog in a pot of cool water and gradually heat the water to the boiling point, it will remain in the pot until it dies. Fassel contends that this is the perfect metaphor for the state of workaholism in our society today.[25]

Whether we are all becoming certifiable workaholics or not (and yes, there is a nationally based Workaholics Anonymous Association), the bottom line is that as a nation we are working more and more and recreating less and less. According to a 2001 survey by Oxford Health Plans, an East Coast health care provider, one in six U.S. employees ends up not taking all of their annual vacation time because of the demands of the job. The survey further pointed out that 34 percent of workers report that they have no downtime on the job; 32 percent don't leave the building at all during the day; 19 percent of respondents said they feel obliged to go to work even when they're ill; 17 percent said it's hard to take time off, even for an emergency; and, 8 percent believe they'd be fired or demoted if they became seriously ill.[26] In another survey, conducted by the *Wall Street Journal*, some workers claim that all too often vacations don't even seem like real vacations. At Dallas-based 7-Eleven Inc., for example, most headquarters employees feel pressured, if not directly ordered or obligated, to take their cell phones and laptops with them on vacation. And, Seattle's RealNetworks, Inc., requires anyone asking for more than ten days off at a time to make the request through a vice president rather than through a manager.[27]

According to Joe Robinson, former editor of an adventure-travel magazine, "we're the most vacation-starved country in the world." There is only one other country with fewer vacation days than America (ten to thirteen) and that is Mexico (six). And what is worse is that in America these vacation days are not required by law but rather are the result of negotiated contracts or custom and tradition. In comparison to the mandated vacation schedules of other industrialized nations, American workers are suffering from a serious leisure lag: Italy, forty-two days; Germany, thirty-five; Sweden, thirty-two; Spain, thirty; Denmark, thirty; Ireland, twenty-eight; and even the work-addicted Japanese, twenty-five mandated vacation days a year.[28]

Financially speaking, all the hours we have put in on the job have not necessarily gone unrewarded. According to the Federal Reserve (January 2000) 12.6 percent of all households earn less than $10,000 annually; 24.8 percent earn between $10,000 and $24,999; 28.8 percent earn between $25,000 and $49,999; 25.2 percent earn between $50,000 and $99,999; and 8.6 percent earn $100,000 or more a year.[29] As of this writing, the median American household income is in excess of $41,000. On average, more working households are doing better than ever before. More of us own homes than at any other time in our history. Two-car families are now the norm. Shopping malls are everywhere, and consumer products are abundant and widely distributed.

We make more than ever before. We own more than ever before. And, of course, we owe more than ever before. The problem is, we work more and more in the manic pursuit to maintain our lives and our lifestyles. The reality is that all too often we have neither the time nor the energy to enjoy the fruits of our labor. As a society, we are suffering from frenzy, frustration, and fatigue. To turn around the words of Thorstein Veblen, we have become a "harried working class" rather than a "leisure class."[30]

Hallmark cards, those almost unnerving barometers of American mores, at one time marketed a series of cards that perhaps all too accurately captures the pace of our lives and the busyness of our days. They were greeting cards for absent working parents to slip under cereal boxes in the morning with the message: "Have a super day at school," or to place on a child's pillow at night: "I wish I were there to tuck you in."[31]

To paraphrase the Bard of Stratford—*Hamlet*, Act 1, Scene 1, Line 67—Me thinks there is something rotten in the state of Denmark!

two

Leisure and Culture
THE IMPORTANCE
OF BEING LAZY

All work and no play make Jack a dull boy.

—James Howell

Anna Quindlen of Newsweek has offered us two apparently con-
tradictory pieces of wisdom about the importance of work in
our lives. (1) "There is nothing so grand in all the world as
watching a person who loves what he does do it."[1] (2) "You
cannot be really first-rate at your work if your work is all you
are."[2] The bridge between these two seemingly disconnected
truths and what puts them into proper perspective, at the individual level, is how we portion out and deal with the rest of our
lives. That is, how we handle our nonwork lives, our time off
the job, our downtime, our leisure. (Better known in the U.K. as
le zḥ´er and in the U.S.A. as lē ´zh er.)

What Quindlen is implying is that to do a job well and
enjoy the job you are doing, you have to be suited for it, like it,
and not do so much of it that you get lost in it, and forget why
you're doing it and/or why it should be done. It's what the
actor George C. Scott meant when he explained why, although

he preferred the stage to films, he would never do a Broadway show for longer than six months: "You can't do a matinee and two supper shows everyday, week in and week out, and still stay fresh enough to bring anything new to the role."

Exaggeration and details aside (matinees are only on Wednesdays and Saturdays and double evening performances occur only on Friday and Saturday nights, if they happen at all), Scott's meaning is right on target. Even when you love the job you're doing, you can't do it all the time without losing something. To do almost anything well, you must have time off from it. Time away from constantly doing it. Time to recover and relax. Time to do something else. Time to just forget about it.

Although Mel Brooks as writer, producer, and director of The Producers, and the recipient of twelve Tony Awards, can pull it off, it's still not considered "politically correct" to quote a Nazi, even a repentant one. Nevertheless, I'm going to anyway. Albert Speer, Third Reich minister of technology and armaments, argues in his memoir, Spandau, that intentions and ideology aside (no small achievement, of course), Hitler's chief failings as a military leader were overextension, overexertion, and fatigue. Hitler, said Speer, especially when the war began to turn against Germany, never seriously rested or recreated or could find any downtime, away time from the all-consuming particulars of the war. He took on too much, said Speer, and micromanaged too much. He got lost in the details, and his fatigue often blinded him to the obvious logic of the situation. History, not so surprisingly, tells us there were other factors in play as well. These were, of course, Hitler's raging paranoia, his all-consuming myopia and narcissism, and his total lack of formal military training. Nevertheless, Speer's insights remain cogent. Fatigue and the frenzy of overstimulation can block objectivity, delimit perspective, and often deaden our ability to calculate and evaluate logically. Vince Lombardi, NFL coach and football legend, is reported to have said that "fatigue makes cowards and fools of us all and more often than not results in mediocrity." Another American legend, Gary Cooper, in a less-than-legendary 1953 film, *Seminole*, perhaps put it most succinctly: "Never decide or do anything when you're tired."

A less controversial student of leadership, James MacGregor Burns, suggests that one of the essential qualities of leadership is to bring a "fresh perspective" to the problem, "to think outside the box," to see beyond the "minutia of excessive details." Effective leadership, suggests Burns in his Pulitzer Prize–winning study *Leadership*, needs to balance "total immersion" in the issues with "time away" from the issues and problems at hand. Rest, recreation, and regular vacations should be part of the job description of all forms of leadership. Working longer and working harder does not mean that a leader or any worker is necessarily working smarter or better. As the reclusive philosopher Baruch Spinoza suggested, in order to gain perspective, we need to step back; insight and wisdom are very often best achieved in moments away from the task at hand.

Robert Reich argues that more of us are more prosperous and better off than ever before. We make more. We do more. We own more. But, he said, there is a price to be paid for this prosperity. Paid work is demanding more of our time, more of our energy, and more and more of our emotional and psychological reserves. He suggests that another big part of the price we pay for our progress and prosperity is that we have lost, if we ever truly understood, the meaning and importance of leisure in our lives.[3]

According to the social commentator Witold Rybczynski, most Americans are so immersed in the pace, meter, and ethos of their workaday lives that they find it hard to distinguish among such key nonwork terms as lazy, recreation, and leisure and often use them more or less interchangeably. This inability, suggests Rybczynski, may not be critical in regard to common usage, but it does delimit and diminish us both as individuals and as a society.[4]

Lazy

Wayne E. Oates, psychologist, pastoral counselor, and the inventor of the term *workaholic*, argues that as a culture we are steadfastly schizophrenic about our understanding of the term *lazy*. On the one hand, in our workaday world of intense competition, productivity, and status seeking, to be called lazy is to be despised by others and often by ourselves as well. "Lazy" is often used as a four-letter word to ridicule individuals who lack energy and effort, or who are slow-moving, sluggish, slothful, or just plain goofing off. To be labeled lazy is to be thought of as immature, undependable, irresponsible, indolent, and/or uselessly idle.[5]

On the other hand, says Oates, we long to be lazy, to do nothing, to be purposely inactive. We crave lazy summer afternoons. We brag about lazy winter weekends or, at the very least, the luxury of "long lazy Sunday mornings with the *New York Times*." In one sense, says Oates, we see being lazy as a status symbol, a badge of honor, a privilege and a right. Although we do not see it as "an inalienable right from birth," we do think of it as a right we have earned by the fruit of our labor.[6] To be rightfully idle, to be righteously lazy, purposeless, with no tasks to do is a direct reflection of our success at work. To openly rest, relax, recuperate, to *redux* (to recover, return to health) without worrying about what others might think is testimony to our success and status as workers. After all, besides being judged by what we do, how much we earn, where we live, and what we own, another index of prestige and pedigree is "acquired time off the job."

Part of the true luxury of "earned laziness" are the bragging rights that come along with being purposefully and publicly lazy. It is a badge of distinction, an emblem of success, without having to say too much about it. It labels us, affords us kudos, and raises our profile in the "pecking order" of our fellow troglodytes. It says to others, "See, I've done so well that I can afford to do nothing at all whenever I so choose!" Citing the historian Sebastian de Grazia, Oates reinforces the "importance of being lazy" as both a private and a public good.

> Perhaps we can judge the inner health of a land by the capacity of its people to do nothing—to lie in a bed, to amble about aimlessly, to sit having a coffee—because whoever can do nothing, letting his thoughts go where they may, must be at peace with himself.[7]

Recreation

We all seek to be idle, to be lazy, to enjoy rest as a natural antidote to the fatigue and frustrations of the job. As U.S. Supreme Court Justice Thurgood Marshall, when asked about his plans after retirement, so prosaically put it, "Sit on my rear end!" But even well practiced lassitude has its limits. No one can remain idle forever, except possibly my son—at least when he was a teenager. After a while, even the benefits of laziness can become a burden or at the very least lead to boredom and the kind of anxiety that results from being excessively idle. All of us naturally seek some form of diversion or recreation. Activities that change the pace, change the place, or change the nature of our usual habits. Activities that effect our enjoyment or relieve our stress. In common parlance, this is what most of us mean by the term *play*.

According to the philosopher Hannah Arendt, from the standpoint of "making a living" every activity which is unconnected to labor and is not necessary either for the life of the individual or the life process of society is subsumed under the term *playfulness*.[8] Play, from the Middle English *plega*, "to leap for joy, to dance, to rejoice, to be glad," is about activity outside the sphere of the customary, the necessary, or the materially useful. The poet Diane Ackerman says "play is a refuge from ordinary life, a sanctuary of the mind, where one is exempt from life's customs, methods, and decrees."[9] Fellow poet Donald Hall suggests that play is about "absorbedness"—"a noun with a lot of verb in it"—which connotes concentration, contentment, loss of self, loss of time, happiness and joy.[10]

For both children and adults, play is about awe, wonder, rapture, and enthusiasm. Play is something we want to do, something we choose to do that is not work, that we enjoy, and that gives us gratification and fun. In play, we drop inhibitions, give ourselves permission to imagine, to be creative, to be curious. Play, like laughter, is an end in itself, something done without any other incentive except for the pleasure involved in the activity itself.[11]

Unfortunately, for too many of us our various forms of recreation and play are really about rehabilitation, recuperation, and recovery rather than rapture and the possibility of the rediscovery of self. This is because, for many of us, our play or diversions are really only momentary distractions from the usual pace of life. They are designed to overcome fatigue, numb awareness, or appease a particular appetite—all for the purpose of reinvigorating and restoring us to the work task at hand. In other words, a lot of what we do, how we spend our time off the job—hobbies, clubs, organizations, going to films, theater, listening to music, working out, friends, vegging out in front of the TV, whatever—is really about taking a break, filling in time, catching up, recharging our batteries, overcoming our fatigue and feelings of stupification so that we go back to the job to endure and earn more.

Revitalization and rejuvenation, not refinement and reformulation, are really at the heart of much of our nonwork activities. For a lot of us, recreation is therapy, a placebo, or an opiate to get us by and keep us going. Even actions, activities, or hobbies that seem wholesome, worthwhile, or of some benefit to the actor can be engaged in for all the wrong reasons—to kill time, to provide a socially acceptable form of anesthetic diversion—and thereby do not constitute true play.

I've played a game called handball for thirty years. I love the sport because it requires a combination of strength, endurance, agility, and quick decision making. Unfortunately these are traits and talents I am woefully deficient in. Over the years I have spent a small fortune on magazines, books, group clinics, and private lessons in an attempt to improve my game. But even with all of this, I remain an erratic and mediocre player. Nevertheless, I play every chance I get for the conditioning effects, because it allows me to be playfully competitive, and because it's a lot of fun.

A number of years ago, I would occasionally play handball before going off to work with a group of men at my local YMCA. One of the guys I was regularly paired with was a solid player who was always looking for a fresh victim. Although I could stay with him for a while, I could never beat him. He was too talented and tough for me, and although my age, he was in much better shape than I was. Besides playing handball every day, he regularly skipped lunch for an aerobics class, and every other evening he ran three to five miles.

One morning over a postgame cup of coffee, I found out that his workout habits were not based on love of the game, middle-age machismo, or the simple pursuit of physical fitness. He said he played a lot of ball and drove himself hard athletically because he was "bored senseless" with his job, he was caught in a "bad marriage," and he needed an outlet to maintain his sanity. He said he had tried drinking for a while, but he just didn't like what the booze did to him. He also said he tried the other "usual male forms" of diversion and escape, but his conscience bothered him too much. So, he said, he had played handball in college and he picked it up again. "Don't get me wrong," he told me, "playing a lot of handball doesn't make the job or home any better. But it gives me something to do, someplace to be, and something to look forward to. Think about it. There are a lot worse ways to keep yourself busy!"

Leisure

Because too many of us live in a world of total work, we think that leisure is at least minimally achieved by the mere absence of work. Because we are so eager to escape the burdens of work, we think that any form of nonwork—quiet time, downtime, doing no-thing in regard to a job time—constitutes some form of rest, recreation, and/or leisure. Well, we're wrong. To be idle, to be without a task, to be doing no-thing are prerequisites but not sufficient conditions for the achievement of genuine leisure.

G. K. Chesterton, English essayist, editor, critic, novelist, lecturer, broadcaster—and, ironically, a card-carrying workaholic—spent a great deal of time and energy writing about the exact nature and necessity of leisure. Chesterton argues, like the *Oxford English Dictionary*, that leisure is about "free time," "time which one can spend as one pleases." The root of the word leisure comes from the Latin *licere*, which means "to be permitted," suggesting that leisure is about unstructured, free-choice time. But, says Chesterton, there are wiser and lesser choices one can make in regard to one's free time. Leisure, he said, can be used to describe three different sorts of things. "The first (and the most common form of leisure) is being allowed to do something (something other than work). The second is being allowed to do anything (anything that engages your interest or desires). And the third is being allowed to do nothing (a noble habit that is both difficult and rare)."[12]

For Chesterton the "noble habit of doing nothing" means to do no practical, utilitarian or quotidian task. He does not mean that leisure is equal to inertia or to do nothing at all. Rather, leisure is the opportunity to do other than that which is necessary or required. To do as one pleases. To be freed from the mundane. To be free to pursue the unusual, the inexplicable, the irrelevant, the interesting, and the idiosyncratic.

According to the psychiatrist Leonard Fagin, the concept of control is the crucial psychological distinction between work and leisure. What characterizes leisure is the feeling, if not the reality, of greater control over one's activity; leisure implies doing what one wants to do with one's "free" or "non-work time." Fagin argues that although work does not imply a total loss of autonomy and control, one's activities at work are never totally arbitrary and without purpose. Rather, they are structured, goal oriented, and, more often than not, supervised and monitored. At the very least, says Fagin, in work one temporarily hands over control to the other agencies. Ostensibly, this sacrifice of control is done in return for financial gain, which offers the possibility of control over one's "non-work time." Conventional wisdom is clear on the matter: leisure is our time; work belongs to another.[13]

Chesterton's own choices and leisure pastimes included an eclectic mix of the unusual and eccentric—sketching, collecting weapons, and playing with the cardboard cutouts of his toy theater. Another famous Englishman, Winston Churchill, had a few eccentric passions of his own. Churchill was both an accomplished painter (on canvas, not walls) and a bricklayer. At Chartwell, his rural estate, he built two cottages, a playhouse, and several walls. Both men were amateurs in the best sense of the word. Amateur comes from the Latin *amare*, which means "to love" and connotes "doing something that you love," "doing something without obligation," "doing something as a dilettante or in a nonprofessional capacity." Both men were convinced that leisure meant time free of the encumbrance of convention, free from "business-busyness," free of the constraints of social obligation and duty.[14]

Josef Pieper, in his cult classic *Leisure: The Basis of Culture*, argues that leisure is a necessary condition for both individual and communal survival, growth, and progress. Pieper claims that because so many of us are addicted, by choice or circumstances, to the idolatry of work, we are not sure of what leisure is, and even worse, in the words of Bertrand Russell, we have been tricked into accepting a life without leisure as normal.[15]

Strictly speaking, for Pieper, leisure is not simply a form of recreation or diversion, nor is it the natural result of rest, relaxation, or amusement. Although, it is necessary to be free of the toil and moil of the everyday burdens of work for it to occur, according to Pieper leisure is primarily a mental set, a psychological orientation, a condition of one's soul or spirit. For Pieper, leisure is an attitude of nonactivity, of not being busy, of inner calm, a commitment to silence, meditation, observation, and letting things be. Leisure is a way of life and not just the inevitable by-product of holidays, spare time, weekends, or a vacation.

> Leisure is a form of silence, of that silence which is the prerequisite of the apprehension of reality . . . For leisure is a receptive attitude of the mind, a contemplative attitude . . .
> Leisure, like contemplation, is of a higher order than the *vita activa* [active life] . . . It is only in and through leisure that the "gate of freedom" is opened and man can escape from the closed circle of that "latent dread and anxiety" . . . the mark of the world of work.[16]

To be leisurely, said Josef Pieper, is a choice. To be leisurely is to be disengaged from the tedium of tasks—to be open, observant, and receptive to issues outside of self and one's immediate needs. Leisure is time given to contemplation, wonder, awe, and the development of ideas. Leisure is about creativity, insight, unregulated thoughts. It is about intellectual activity, but not intellectual work or utilitarian problem solving. It is about desire, wonder, and unbridled curiosity. For Thomas Aquinas, leisure is the vehicle, the necessary condition for the *vita contemplative* (life of the mind), which is the "noblest mode of human life" and the primary means by which we transcend the limits of the human condition.[17]

Like Aristotle before him, Pieper believed that leisure is the catalyst for culture and the development of philosophy, theology, poetry, and the arts. Culture, for Pieper, is all that which is beyond the immediate sphere of wants and needs. Culture is that which is not absolutely necessary, useful, or utilitarian, but that which ultimately defines us as a species or a group.

In both the *Nicomachean Ethics* and the *Politics* Aristotle argued that leisure is the center point about which everything revolves. It is leisure, says Aristotle, that is the source of distinction between *artes liberales* (fine arts, liberal arts, an end in itself) and the *artes serviles* (physical and domestic work, for a practical purpose). For Aristotle it is leisure that distinguishes between a high and low calling, between menial and mental tasks, between physical necessity and intellectual curiosity.

Of course, Aristotle had a rather skewed and parochial perspective on exactly who should work and who should enjoy leisure. To the ancient Greeks, whose physical labor was, in large part, done by slaves, work brutalized the mind and made men unfit for the practice of gentlemanly virtues. The Greeks regarded work as a curse, a drudgery and a heavy-hearted activity. Plutarch in his chapter on Pericles remarks that no well-born man would want to be the craftsman Phidias. While a gentleman enjoys the contemplation of the sculptor's masterpieces, he himself would never consider using a hammer and chisel and being covered with dust, sweat, and grime.[18] The Greeks felt that work enslaved the worker, chained him to the will of others, and corrupted his soul. Work by its very nature inhibited the use of reason and thereby impeded the search for the ultimate ends of life. Work was accepted not as an end in itself but as a means by which some might be freed to pursue higher goals. Aristotle declared that just as the goal of war was peace, so the object of work was leisure. Leisure meant activity pursued free of compulsion or desire for gain, free for the contemplation of philosophical issues and truths. Aristotle would have found the Protestant work ethic's commitment to "work as duty" and "work for work sake alone" completely foreign concepts. Aristotle saw physical work as a burden which he had no duty to bear. He himself never worked, accepting the slavery of others because it freed him for leisure and the "work of the mind."[19]

Although Josef Pieper's definition of leisure is drawn from classic, medieval, and Victorian sources, his analysis remains, at least in principle, at the core of two contemporary cultural institutions: vacations and the observation of the Sabbath. In Latin the word for vacation is *vacare*, "to be empty, nonoccupied," "to suspend activity," "to do nothing." Work represents the everyday routine, and vacations are temporary interruptions.[20] On vacations we turn aside, go in the opposite direction, vacate ourselves from our usual course or purpose. Vacations connote downtime, choice, freedom, personal discretion, and activities an individual engages in for his or her own purposes and pleasures. Vacations are seen as an antidote to work. They are medicine, a remedy for counteracting the effects of labor. The psychologist Wayne E. Oates believes that vacations offer us an opportunity to "empty ourselves of our multiple roles in life." Vacations allow us to be away from the job, to change the patterns of our day, to alter our routine, to reconfigure our actions and habits, to rediscover ourselves.[21]

Although it is not true for everyone, we commonly associate vacations or vacationing with traveling. In traveling, we take ourselves outside of ourselves, our normal life, our usual patterns. In traveling we seek delight, diversion, and differences. In traveling, there is the opportunity or potential for solitude, speculation, wonder, and awe.

The Chinese philosopher Lin Yutang said that the true purpose of travel is not rest or recovery but rediscovery and renewal. In travel, he said, we "should become lost and unknown." He chides vacationers who bring along with them handfuls of letters of introduction so that they will become known wherever they are. Anonymity, he claims, is far better. To have no fixed hours, no inquisitive neighbors, no mail, no

e-mails, telephone calls, or faxes offers us a chance to expand our horizons and reevaluate and possibly redefine who we are. For Lin Yutang, vacations are opportunities to rediscover our basic humanness apart from our accustomed personas and roles in life.[22]

Within the Jewish tradition, the Sabbath (in Hebrew, *Shabbat*, "to rest") is Saturday, the seventh day of the week, a day specifically set aside for rest and religious observance. According to the Book of Exodus, the Fourth Commandment enjoined the Jews: "Six days you shall labor, and do all your work; but the seventh day is a Sabbath to the Lord your God, in it you shall not do any manner of work." In most Christian traditions, the Sabbath is the first day of the week, Sunday (in Latin, *dies solis*, "day of the sun"). It is observed as a holy day and a holiday in commemoration of the resurrection of Christ. Although the terms *Sunday* and *Sabbath* are not strictly synonymous, they both connote the imperative to set aside work for the purposes of celebration, recreation, and religious festivity. Moreover, the notion of a "day free from labor" is a cross-cultural historical constant that can be found in numerous ethnic and religious groups—Greeks, Romans, Chinese, Hindus, Buddhists, Taoists, Muslims—and even Marxists.

For the observant Jew, there are in excess of thirty-nine specific Talmudic prohibitions against work on the Sabbath. Since God created all in just six days and rested on the seventh, for men to work or to create on the Sabbath would make them guilty of, at least, vanity and hubris and, possibly, sacrilege. (In the ancient texts, tasks such as sowing, plowing, reaping, threshing, and winnowing are among those things expressly prohibited, as are grinding, sifting, weaving, hunting, and slaughtering, building, hammering, and transporting. And there are, of course, by way of analogy a whole host of modern prohibitions such as not turning on an electric light, watching TV, or using the phone.) But at the heart of Sabbath prohibitions lies a larger and more humanly profound message. The Sabbath is a day of celebration and joy. On the Sabbath, the good Jew is required by rule to be thankful for all of God's goodness and to celebrate that goodness with one's friends and family with wine, fun, and play. In other words, they are required to show their gratitude for life by giving themselves over to leisure and play.

The Christian version of this Commandment reads: "Remember to keep holy the Lord's Day." Within the Catholic Church it was a mortal sin (punishable by eternal damnation) not to attend church or to do any unnecessary or avoidable work on a Sunday. It was also considered a venial sin (a blot on one's soul, but not one warranting absolute damnation) to go shopping on a Sunday. Within all Christian sects, the Lord's Day was a day committed to prayer, leisure, and family.

The theologian Matthew Fox observes that the purpose behind all these various religious rules and restrictions was to disconnect us from the world of work and the usual rhythms of life in order to remind ourselves of higher values and greater purposes. Jesus told us, says Fox, "that the Sabbath is for people, not the people for Sabbath." Sabbath is not about the rules, per se. It is about wonder, joy, and delight. It is about the "sanctity of time," the "architecture of time," and the "architect of time." It is about marveling at the complexity and mystery of reality. It is an interlude from the tyranny of the commonplace. It is being able to do something without a why. It is the celebration of the obvious and the obtuse. It is about relaxation, effortlessness. It is a pause, a moment for a brief spiritual vacation and renewal.[23] Sabbath, suggests Fox, is space and time created to say yes to spirituality, sensuality, sexuality, prayer, rest, song, and delight. Only when we cease our daily labor do we have time for love, friendship, God, and ourselves. In celebrating Sabbath we are saying to the world, "Today I'm going to pamper my soul."[24]

In the Middle Ages, Thomas Aquinas wrote: "It is necessary for the perfection of human society that there should be men [people] who devote their lives to contemplation."[25] He believed leisure was essential to civilization because leisure allows us the serenity to recognize the differences between the mysterious and the mundane. Leisure offers us openness to ourselves and others. Leisure allows us to muse, meditate, and wonder, to find perspective beyond the immediate and the necessary. Leisure allows us to be more than workers; to no longer be mere functionaries of the system; to be "unfettered from the process of work."[26]

The bottom line seems fairly obvious. We are marked, molded, identified, and known to ourselves and others by what we do for a living (work) and how we play (leisure). The question is, have we made the equation too one-sided? Is the world too busy for genuine leisure anymore? Are we all too addicted, too dependent, too needful of work to step away from it, even for a while? Why is it that for so many of us, leisure has been reduced to recuperation and indulgence? Why is it that so many of us have neither the time, the discipline, nor the tolerance for quiet, solitude, and wonder? Why is it that so many of us think that constant busyness and noise are normal, and that silence is a void waiting to be filled? Why is it that so many of us need to "fill in" and "fill up" all of our time both on and off the job? Why is it that so many of us work at play as hard as or harder than we do at work?

three

Vacations and Traveling

I've often been asked as an adventure magazine editor whether there are any exciting places left in a world that's already mapped. The answer is: plenty, because the real adventure isn't about boldly going where no man has gone before; it's about going where you've never been. . . . It's about the vast landscape of incognita territory within each of us, revealed through the magic of the journey.

—*Joe Robinson*

According to family folklore, except for a few brief honeymoons, none of us had taken a real vacation until 1954. That summer, my father, mother, aunt, uncle, and myself piled into my dad's brand new, sky-blue Oldsmobile Rocket 88 (eight cylinders, 320 horsepower, hydromatic drive, oversized whitewall tires, AM-radio, and no air conditioner!), and we drove cross-country from Chicago to Boise to Los Angeles to the Grand Canyon, and back to Chicago again—all in two weeks, to see family, friends, and the wild, wild west! It was like undergoing two weeks of root canal surgery. Surprisingly, we all got along amazingly well. The problems were not with the personalities involved, but the amenities of the road.

You've got to remember that these were the days before chain restaurants, chain motels, and an interlinking chain of interstate highways with restrooms and information kiosks regularly dotting the roadway. The song may have said, "Get your kicks on Route 66," but kicks were pretty hard to come by when the only thing out there for hundreds of miles at a time was an occasional Stuckeys or a Texaco gas station with dirty bathrooms and a Coca-Cola machine which was invariably empty or broken.

And then there was the problem of lodging. The hotels (or

motor courts as I believe they were then called) that were available were either tiny cubicles, freestanding cabins or huts, or something right out of Alfred Hitchcock—Mrs. Bates' Hotel/Motel, "Travelers Welcome!" Believe me, Chevy Chase's odyssey to Wally World with his collective menagerie had nothing on us!

Since the 1950s, generations of American families have been taking cross-country vacations just as we did. According to the American Automobile Association, motoring remains the number one way families travel while on vacation. There are, however, some important differences and nuances between motoring then and now.

To begin with, the sedans of yesterday have been replaced with vans and SUVs. Air conditioning is now considered standard, AM-radio has been augmented by FM-radio, cassette players, CD players, and, in trucks and vans, TV monitors and VCR players. Rest stops with clean restrooms are at regular intervals on President Eisenhower's legacy of 43,000-plus miles of stoplight-free roads linking every major city in America. Restaurants catering to the needs of families on the go can be found at almost every exit. And, finally, motel chains are everywhere. They all may be cookie-cutter in design, but most of them are safe, clean, reasonably priced, and convenient. (Of course, certain things never change. Both then and now, each room comes with its own copy of the Gideon Bible in either a standard or pocket-size book format.)

The other major differences, I think, came about because of changes in the structure of families, job demands, kids' schedules, and finances. For example, the standard two-week vacation is a thing of the past. Most road trips now range from two to five days, and of course cover shorter distances. Most trips are to a specific location and not simply an attempt to fulfill Dinah Shore's commercial jingle from the early 1950s: "See the USA in your Chevrolet, America is waiting for you to call. Drive your Chevrolet across the USA, America is the greatest land of all."[1]

And yet, for all these differences, there are some things that remain the same: kids asking, "Are we there yet?"; fights over radio stations, music selection, and volume; mothers yelling, "Can't you two play nicely together?"; and—the dire warning of dads—"Listen, if I have to, I'll turn this car around right now! Believe me, I will do it! And, you will be sorry!" (Yeah, right!)

Cruising cross-country to California in my dad's Oldsmobile was the last family vacation we ever took, and the very last vacation I was ever on until I took my family in the early 1970s to Colorado in the claustrophobic confines of a Volkswagen Beetle. (Isn't it funny how ontogeny reduplicates phylogeny?) After my childhood California extravaganza, vacations to me meant being out of school, staying at grandma's, playing baseball almost every day, going to a double feature on Wednesdays, taking the bus to the beach, and every once in a while, going on a picnic in a local forest preserve.

My parents always took their vacation time, but they didn't do anything with it. We stayed pretty much close to home. My dad had more days off than my mom. But most of the time he worked a second job, or played golf (his one great passion), or did chores around the house. None of my grandparents went on vacation either. The only traveling they had ever done was when they migrated to this country from Italy. In fact, my father and both my grandfathers complained that the only time they had traveled—for my dad to fight in World War II and for my grandfathers in third-class steerage from Naples to New York—they hated it. So why, they asked, would they choose to do it again? The only member of my family to travel was my Uncle Joe. He and my Aunt Theresa took every chance they could to go on vacation. I thought them exotic world travelers. At least three times a year, they went to Wisconsin to fish!

In some sense the history of my family reflects the history and evolution of vacationing in this country. Vacations are both a private event and a social institution. As a private event, they say something about us at the level of class, cash, and culture. The same must be said of vacation as a social institution. When vacations become part of a society, they say something about the pedigree of that society at the level of education, finance, infrastructure, social enlightenment, and civil rights. Vacations do not occur in a vacuum. They are the result and the expression of other economic, political, and philosophical values.

As Professor Cindy S. Aron has argued in her insightful and informative study *Working at Play: A History of Vacations in America*, vacations tell us much about the society and even more about the vacationer. "More than just yearly rituals . . . ," argues Aron, "vacations are also exercises in self-definition. In affording time away from the demands of everyday life, vacations disclose what people choose to do rather than are required to do."[2]

For the most part, until well into the twentieth century, travel of any kind was a restricted prerogative of the wealthy or an absolute necessity for the desperate and the poor. Whether motivated by desire or need, traveling by any means (ship, rail, or coach) was arduous, complicated, slow, and costly. One needed a strong stomach, a hearty constitution, steady sea legs, patience, and goodly amounts of cash to endure the ordeal. Even in the later part of the nineteenth century, in the age of advanced sail (clipper ships and combination steam and sail vessels), few individuals gladly embraced or eagerly sought out a two-to-four-week transatlantic crossing unless the motivation was necessity, business, or the prospect of high adventure.

None of this means, of course, that everyone stayed home. The seventeenth, eighteenth, and nineteenth centuries were, according to the historian Daniel J. Boorstin, all part of the "great age of discovery and exploration." Led, first, by explorers and adventurers, followed by soldiers, missionaries, and merchants—as well as economic misfits and political and religious malcontents—hundreds of thousands sought out the "New World" for a chance at a new beginning. In 1565, Pedro

Menendez de Auiles, a Spanish smuggler and soldier of fortune with a ragtag army of 1,500, built the first permanent European settlement on American soil at St. Augustine, Florida. In 1620 the good ship *Mayflower* deposited its 101 seasick and disoriented passengers on the rocky shores of Plymouth, Massachusetts. And between 1815 and 1914, more than 30 million Europeans left their homelands to settle in the "New World." It was by far the greatest mass movement in human history.[3]

During these years, the trail of traffic was not just one-way and not only limited to the purposes of commerce and migration. There was also a small but steady reverse flow of travelers from the "New World" back to the "Old." In the main, most traveled for business, but increasingly after the Civil War more and more traveled for culture and play. For those afflicted with wanderlust and possessing the wherewithal to act on it, Boston and New York were regular points of departure for Europe and other ports of call. If one were looking for a typical family of nineteenth-century travelers, I believe the Henry James family of New York, Massachusetts, Rhode Island, and points beyond would do nicely.

Henry James Sr. was the son and heir of a successful businessman who left him with an income of $10,000 a year. Freed of the necessity of earning a living, Henry pursued philosophy, religion, and the international education of his five children, the two oldest being William James (the philosopher who wrote like a novelist) and Henry James Jr. (the novelist who wrote like a philosopher).

From the time they were toddlers to teenagers, Henry Sr. shepherded his children along with his wife and a gaggle of nannies, relatives, and friends, plus steamer trunks and boxes of books, back and forth across the Atlantic (at least ten times) in the pursuit of special classes, tutors, exhibitions, and historic points of interest. Although the family usually traveled first-class and had the financial means to insulate themselves from the usual indignities and inefficiencies of travel, according to family letters and diaries, the children loathed the transatlantic passages and considered them an ordeal rather than an opportunity. Only the stubborn determination and the deep pockets of Henry Sr. kept them at it.

Today, thanks to a long series of economic and technological innovations, you no longer have to be a scion of wealth or a sadist to take your family to Europe or other faraway places on a regular basis. (During the economic good times of the Clinton years, round trip New York to London by air was just over $400 a ticket. And Chicago to Cape Town could be had for $1,600.) In general, Americans' appetite for traveling has grown exponentially. It is estimated that we spend in excess of half a trillion dollars a year on vacations, and the international airlines industry claims to handle an estimated 670 million passengers a year.[4]

For our immediate purposes, let's set aside the small fraction of the population that sailed the high seas in pursuit of business and commerce or leisure and play, and briefly look at how most Americans have historically sought to use their vacation time. To begin with, prior to the 1850s, few Americans would have used the word *vacation* to describe pleasure travel or time devoted to recreation, recuperation, or play.

According to Cindy Aron, most Americans used "vacation" or "vacation time" to refer to students' or teachers' breaks from school or college. It was only in the mid-1850s that "vacation" crept into private use and published works to describe something more than just "time off." For example, an 1855 editorial in the *New York Times* titled "Vacations for Businessmen" urged men to "grasp at less and enjoy more." Incessant work, the editorial warned, would result in a life "sans health, sans stomach, sans capacity for all better and higher things."[5]

But more than just a shift in terminology, the mid–nineteenth century saw a shift in how Americans looked at play. Our Puritan heritage saddled us with a legacy that denigrated amusement, pleasure, and play. Recreation, said our Puritan forefathers, is something that restores a person to better work and service. Amusement left people wasted and exhausted. Amusement was "pleasure for pleasure's sake alone." Scripture, they claimed, endured recreation but forbade amusement. As a certified curmudgeon, Thomas MacAulay, pointed out: "The Puritan hated bear-baiting not because it gave pain to the bear, but because it gave pleasure to the spectators."[6] Eventually, of course, the slow decline of strict Calvinist ideas led to a change in our attitude regarding recreation and amusement and to a new "cultural permission" to play.[7]

An 1848 article in the Unitarian magazine Christian Examiner argued that "amusements under the plan of Providence, form an essential part of the great system of influence by which human faculties are trained. . . . A sufficient reason for participating in them is that they give pleasure."[8] Again, in 1848 the prominent Congregationalist minister Horace Bushnell preached that "no creature lives that must not work and may not play." Aron interprets Bushnell's message to read: "people work because they must, because prudence impels" and they play because they must as well. Play, for Bushnell, came from "a fund of life that wants to expend itself." Bushnell saw work as an "activity for an end," while play was an "activity as an end." Bushnell thus challenged the reigning "work ethic" that found play acceptable only when it "prepares [us] for new scenes of labor and usefulness!"[9]

Of course, no matter what one's theology, vacations of any kind, under any rubric, and the pursuit of pleasure and play in any form were dependent upon the financial wherewithal to allow for the suspension of work. In other words, as Cindy Aron clearly argues, for a long time in this society only the wealthy and the prominent could actually take a vacation and pursue play. To paraphrase Ernest Hemingway, the rich have always been different from us. They've got a lot more money, and a lot more options, too!

Long before an American middle class existed at all, a tiny number of eighteenth-century elites made their way to a handful of springs and seaside resorts for the purpose of rest, recuperation, and relaxation. In the nineteenth century, a slightly expanded privileged elite sought out vacations at posh and very exclusive watering holes both for the purposes of pleasure and play and as a demonstration of their affluence, social standing, and sophistication. In other words, one went to Saratoga Springs, New York, or Berkeley Springs, Virginia to be amused and entertained and, of course, to be seen. The ability to take a vacation, to take time off, to travel, to be seen, was a statement to oneself and others about one's class and social place.

Although the sacred sanctuaries of the elite remained relatively unsullied by the touch or appearance of commoners or clerks, from the middle of the nineteenth through the middle of the twentieth century there has been a steady democratization of vacations starting with the emergence of the middle class and then passing down this privilege to the lower working classes. As Cindy Aron correctly argues, the history of vacations in America is a reflection of the history of America.

As we became an urban society based on industry rather than agriculture, with a growing and increasingly sophisticated transportation network, what resulted was a general increase in prosperity, more free time, and the creation of a large middle class. These changes allowed both a new vacationing public and new vacationing places to develop and take shape.[10]

Just as the privileged elite saw vacations as a social perk and a badge of honor, so did the middle class. Vacationing became one of the central accoutrements of middle-class refinement and status. According to Cindy Aron:

> Historians have determined various ways in which middle class Victorians distinguished themselves from members of the working class: the nature of their non-manual employment, their urban residential patterns, their adoption of a set of values that

privileged domesticity and privacy, their embrace of refined manners and the trappings of respectability, and their behavior as consumers. I argue that vacationing become another critically important marker of middle class status. Middle class men and women not only claimed the privilege of vacationing, but also made that privilege into a middle class entitlement. By the turn of the twentieth century the middle class had established vacationing as a requirement for its physical health and for its spiritual and emotional well-being as well.[11]

The arrival of vacations as a mass phenomenon for the working class did not take hold until the mid-1930s. And although many reformers saw it as a simple matter of justice, many who advocated vacations for the working class were motivated by practical and not by philanthropic reasons. Social critics and businessmen alike argued that it made good sense to rest both the workers and the equipment in order to guarantee the best possible results. After all: "The human machine, like its mechanical namesake, needs a period of rest and recuperation in order to stay fit."[12]

Aron points out that the "kindheartedness" of other reformers was also less than purely altruistic in its motivation.

> Hoping to stabilize their work force and discourage unionization, a few progressive companies began to consider plans to improve the quality of workers' lives. A small minority of forward-looking welfare capitalists argued that showers, clean washrooms, dining rooms, company picnics and vacations would increase workers loyalty, raise productivity, and decrease the appeal of labor unions. Happy workers, they suggested, were more productive workers.[13]

Whether or not the workforce was generally happier and more productive because of their vacation time off the job is hard to determine. But what is clear is that after Americans had endured the Great Depression and survived World War II, vacations and vacationing became an entrenched part of their way of life. While certainly not every worker took exotic trips to faraway places, knowing that they had "time off" coming to them played an important part in maintaining their mental well-being.

Safari is a Swahili word meaning "journey" or "to travel," but it has come to mean so very much more. Imbued with a sense of the exotic, the word has today become symbolic of something far more romantic. It evokes images of adventure and stylish indulgence as portrayed by actors Meryl Streep and Robert Redford in the 1985 film version of Karen Blixen's *Out of Africa*. Although a good number of us do take "high-end" trips, the vast majority just go on vacation and not on safari. And although our tastes on vacations range from the pedestrian to the posh, most of us settle for the "golden mean" in hopes of getting the biggest bang for our vacation bucks.

But whether we literally head off on a safari or simply set out to see the sites of Williamsburg, Virginia, what we are all secretly seeking is an adventure. Of course, the adventure we are seeking is not necessarily the overhyped Hollywood version of something "unusual, stirring, expensive, and, of course, romantic." I think the adventure we more realistically desire conforms to the word's original meaning in Latin: *adventura, advenire*, "that which happens without design; chance, happenstance, luck!"[14]

What most of us would gladly settle for on vacation is far from exotic and is definitely not dependent on the daring deeds of Indiana Jones. We want a break from the normal routine: different, interesting, and pleasant surroundings; a couple of laughs; a few decent meals that we don't have to prepare for ourselves; and, hopefully, walking away from it all without the feeling of being financially ripped off or rudely treated along the way. It may not be the sum total of the American Dream that our Founding Fathers envisioned, but it sure goes a long way to fulfill at least a part of it: the pursuit of Happiness!

Since World War II, cars, trains, buses, and planes have changed how and when we travel and where we travel to. Convenient means of transportation meant that the vacationing public " no longer needed months of free time or buckets of money to travel."[15] Of course in the last twenty-five years some things have changed. For example, except for short-distance commuting, trains are really no longer in the "long haul" passenger business; and, rightly or wrongly, buses are, for most travelers, considered déclassé and the transportation vehicle of last resort. According to the American Automobile Association, what has not changed in decades is that 80 percent of all Americans who go on vacation drive. Driving remains the number one way to travel up to a thousand miles away from home.[16]

Anyone who has been near a major airport in the summer knows that aviation is the commercial backbone of not just local but global public transportation and travel. The price of gas, the wear and tear on the car, the wear and tear of small children on your psyche, and the fewer number of days we go on vacation have led more and more vacationers (married or single, with or without children) to consider flying a necessity, not an option. There are, of course, trade-offs: security checks, long delays, overbooking, cramped seating, bad food (airline food—a true oxymoron that cannot be eclipsed even by Enron's recent contribution to the term *business ethics*), and lost luggage, but nobody ever said progress didn't come at a price.

So where do we all go when we go on our private or familial odysseys? Not so surprisingly, an awful lot of us are pretty pedestrian in the use of our vacation time. It has been my experience that if you randomly survey a hundred people about how they spend their vacations the answers you will get are not scientific, and not always exactly the same, but they conform to a strikingly consistent pattern. Ten percent will gleefully report about doing something incredibly exotic: flying to Cape Town,

South Africa, to go cage diving with great white sharks; sixteen days trekking through Tanzania; or a rafting trip down the Sepik River in Papua, New Guinea. Another 10 percent will report that they did nothing on their vacation. That is, due to lack of interest or lack of funds, instead of taking an exotic trip, they did some chores around the house, took a trip to the zoo, took in a few museums, and spent a long day and night at their closest Six Flags amusement park.

About 40 percent of those polled will tell you that they had a wonderful time on their vacations even if their destinations of choice were not sites "where no man has ever gone before." These are the folks—"not that there is anything wrong with their choices," to cite Jerry Seinfeld—who help maintain camping out as our number one outdoor vacation activity.[17] These are the folks for whom Disneyland and Disney World are the family vacation destinations of choice. Without children, of course, the adult version of Disneyland is Las Vegas. And for salty silver-haired seniors, it would be Branson, Missouri, where Andy Williams sings "Moon River" at three supper shows nightly. And, lest we forget, for those who love country and blue grass music, there's the Dolly Parton theme park, Dollywood in Pigeon Forge, Tennessee.

These are the individuals, couples, and families who go on the grand tour of our national treasures and sacred sites: the Grand Canyon, Niagara Falls, Mammoth Cave in Kentucky, Washington, Boston, Mount Vernon, Monticello, and Gettysburg. These are the folks who attend sports camps, Shakespeare festivals, and/or Bible study camps. These are the people who try to make it to Europe every third year. These are the hard-core vacationers and tourists who make detailed plans and carefully manage their budgets so that they can take an annual vacation. These are the people who help maintain the collective corporate coffers of the travel industry. And let's give credit where credit is due: these are the people who, though their tastes and destination preferences vary widely, genuinely enjoy traveling. These are the people who hunger for vacation out of inclination, addiction, or desire.

And then there's the surprising 40 percent of us who report visiting family and friends on their vacations. On reflection, perhaps we really shouldn't be shocked by this statistic. Going to see loved ones has historically always been a major reason for traveling. And now, given the fluidity of our lives, our mobility, our multiple job changes, more and more of us live away from our families and our friends because they are scattered about everywhere. So naturally, our vacation time may be the only opportunity we have to get together.

Going to see grandma and grandpa, or spending a week with your brother or best friend from college, does not, of course, mean you do nothing else but spend time with them. Visitors usually end up doing a lot of the stuff that tourists usually do—dinners out, shopping, a little sightseeing. The main problem that was reported to me by a number of people who regularly take "family-visit vacations" is what one of them called "vacation- interruptus" or "vacation-incompletus!" That is, going to see family and friends is a vacation of sorts—you're someplace else, you're doing things, you're having fun—but you're constantly trying to balance your wants and desires with those of others. Because of all this and the sheer numbers involved in the project, the first casualty is usually the possibility of anything resembling "spontaneity" or "adventure." Moreover, the concepts of silence, solitude, and rest rarely enter into the equation.

Putting aside my limited survey, I have also found a growing number of people for whom vacations are anything but pedestrian. The past few decades have seen the rise of adventure travel, ecotravel, and archaeological travel, and now there are vacations that "take you to the limit"—extreme sports vacations. What defines an extreme sport? While there is no exact definition, it doesn't take a genius to figure out that all of them have an above-average propensity to result in death, injury, or maiming. Here are just a few examples: rock climbing, bungee jumping, white-water rafting, base jumping [B-A-S-E, an acronym for parachutists jumping off buildings, antennas, spans (bridges), and earth (cliffs)], bridge swinging, street luge, downhill roller blading, surfing in typhoonlike swells, skiing/snowboarding in avalanche country, and aerobatic parachuting.

Although extreme sports can be a local weekend activity (e.g. parachuting), many of them require time and travel (mountain climbing, skiing) and therefore, most extreme sport athletes dedicate their vacation time to their sport of choice.[18] Extreme sports is about pushing boundaries, taking risks, leaving safety behind to leap into the void. Extreme sports is about a radical rush of adrenaline. It's about forgetting about standards of safety. It's about not being cerebral. It's about *not having control* over the elements. It's not about winning, it's about *not losing, not dying*. It's about elevating risk to the extreme. It's about living through the experience. Simply, it's about the afterglow pleasure of survival.

Clearly, extreme sports vacations are not for the faint of heart. The psychologist Frank Farley of Temple University suggests that the rise of extreme sports is a direct reflection of two human characteristics that also have a predominant role in forming our national character. That is, we are a nation of risk takers and we hate being bored so much that we will take outrageous chances to challenge ourselves and overcome the tedium of monotonous regularity.[19]

As we function in the new millennium, I do not think that Americans will embark on a national orgy of thrill seeking and risk taking, but I do understand why so many of us are drawn to it: it's a combination of the thrill of the unknown, novelty, dancing with danger, and the irresistible possibility of the joy of play—no matter what the downside. We are, after all, curious creatures and thrill seekers. According to Eric Perlman, a mountaineer and filmmaker specializing in extreme sports: "Every human being with two legs, two arms is sometime going to wonder how fast, how strong, how enduring he or she is. We are designed to experiment or die."[20]

Hey, football is for weaklings! Why do they need all those pads? Naked bungee jumping, anyone?

Although the concept of vacations is part and parcel of our general cultural expectations, it is not a reality in the life of every worker. According to a 2001 report by the American Family Institute of New York, one-quarter of the American workforce does not take a regular vacation; two-thirds of people who earn $10,000 or less a year take less than one week off per year; and, day workers, who regularly experience "enforced time off" (not hired for the day) take zero planned vacation days off. And let's not forget George Will's assertion that 40 percent of working Americans work even when they are ostensibly at play, remaining in "daily contact with their offices, by e-mail, from their cabins, by cell phones from their canoes."[21]

The American Family Institute claims that according to this survey what results from no vacation time or too little vacation has immediate and long-term consequences both for the employee and the employer: stress, burnout, lack of focus, increased mistakes, diminished creativity, troubled relationships on and off the job, disruption of sleeping patterns, and health problems.[22]

Garrison Keillor, National Public Radio superstar and official spokesman for the "town that time forgot," Lake Wobegon, Minnesota, recently wrote an essay complaining about spending too much of his life working. Back when he was a kid, said Keillor, he spent his summers picking potatoes at a neighbor's farm. It was dusty, body-aching, boring work, but he kept at it because he was ashamed and afraid to complain or quit. He had been told that work was a challenge, a duty, and a demonstration of manliness. He was warned that if he quit work, his life would lose meaning and purpose and he would be unable to bear the shame. So, he said, he spent a lot of years dutifully picking potatoes in one form or another.

Finally, however, after achieving fame, fortune, success, and open-heart surgery, he's begun to change his mind.

> It's a lovely life, doing nothing. God never intended for me to work hard. I can see that now. My true calling is to live unencumbered and follow the fleeting impulses of my heart and take a nap around 2 P.M. whether I want to or not. I worked hard for years out of plain fear and ignorance and also to impress women and have the funds to take them to restaurants that serve poached salmon with a light saffron sauce on a bed of roses and then bring them home to Tara and when they say, "Wow! What a big house you have!" to say, "Come in and let me show you my art." [23]

Joe Robinson, former editor of the now (sadly) defunct adventure-travel magazine *Escape*, completely agrees with Keillor. We have to work less to be more, says Robinson. In this society we perversely allow "downtime for machinery for maintenance and repair, but we don't allow it for the employees." Americans' most hazardous work-related illness, says Robinson, is vacation deficit disorder or vacation starvation. [24]

Mind you, Robinson, entrepreneur and business owner himself, is not against the work ethic per se. It's the crazed, psychotic overwork ethic, says Robinson, that needs a pink slip. So, he and his fellow workers at the magazine formed a committee called Work to Live. The purpose of the committee was to gather as many signatures as possible to present to the U.S. Congress to prove that there is an enthusiastic constituency for working to live, not just living to work. Robinson's battle cry is one we've all, sorta, heard before: *Workers and travelers of America, Unite! We have nothing to lose but our stress!* [25]

Escape's petition for federally required vacation time was nonpartisan and elegantly simple.

Dear United States Congress:

We the undersigned urge you to amend the Fair Labor Standards Law so that every American who has worked at a job for at least a year gets three weeks paid leave, increasing to four weeks after three years—by federal law, as Europeans do.

In a recent interview Robinson told me that in May 2002 he had presented 50,000 signatures to the labor staffs of Senator Ted Kennedy (Massachusetts) and Representative Henry A. Waxman's (California). Now, says Robinson, all of his efforts have shifted to lobbying Congress to make required vacations the law of the land. "The key point to keep in mind," says Robinson, "is that we're the only industrialized nation without a minimum paid leave law. Furthermore," he argues, "the lack of legitimization via a law is largely responsible for the squirminess people feel when they're on vacation, and for all the stalling, canceling, and abbreviating of vacations!"

According to Robinson a Work to Live law would:

- Stipulate minimum paid leave of three weeks for anyone who has worked at a job for over a year, increasing to four weeks after three years
- Protect employees against any retaliation for taking all the vacation coming to them, and end the fear of replacement, demotion, or promotion fallout from taking a vacation
- Protect against employers stalling or chilling vacations with chronic cancellations
- Prevent vacations from shrinking when an employee changes jobs. You will always get three weeks after you spend a year at a job.
- Provide that after three months with a company and up through the first year an employee would receive a pro rated share of vacation. For example, at six months you would get 1.5 weeks off.

Individuals wishing to stay informed or add their support to the Work to Live campaign can visit Robinson's website at www.worktolive.info.

In the summer of 2001, before the horrors of September 11 and its terrible aftermath, the nation was scandalized by the behavior of its new president, George W. Bush. Thankfully, Mr. Bush did not raise our collective eyebrows for any of the reasons his predecessor regularly shocked us. But what he did, did indeed shock and surprise us! He went on vacation for a month! Of course, the papers, the pundits, and the pollsters had a field day with it. "For an *employee* who's been on the job just eight months, George W. Bush certainly is not shy about using his vacation benefits," chirped the *Chicago Tribune*.[26] "Most of us," declared one slightly outraged radio commentator, "get a week off after one year, two weeks after two, and if we work for a, so called, benevolent company, maybe we get three weeks after ten years on the job! So what's with him?"[27] A Gallup poll found that 48 percent of Americans thought that "the President should not take more than three weeks (of vacation)."[28] And lots of other people, in my own informal poll, told me that the presidency was too important a job to take thirty days off. Actually he revised his plans and took only 27days. (Question: Doesn't anybody remember Jimmy Carter? He was, and is, a great man, the 2002 winner of the Nobel Prize for Peace, but he was not an effective president. Part of the reason, was that he micromanaged everything. He worked long hours every day and never took a vacation if he could avoid it.)

The joke is, of course, that President Bush was, in some sense, on vacation in name only. Yes, he left Washington and went to his Texas ranch. Yes, he played golf with his father and predecessor, George H. Bush. And, yes, he had some friends over for a barbecue and to watch a ballgame. But at the same time, as president of the United States, custom and statute required that he be briefed daily on domestic and international affairs. He always has with him at least a skeleton staff of advisers and aides who bring him work that has to be done. And, I believe, as commander in chief of the armed forces, he is obligated to travel with a military attaché who has access to our central military command center should the president need to act on a military emergency.

Let's be honest, the president's vacation was at best "a working vacation." He spent a little time cutting brush and doing chores around his ranch. He put in a couple of hours pounding nails for Habitat for Humanity. He went to New Mexico for the first day of school. He made a nationally televised speech on stem cell research. He pressed the flesh with locals around Waco, Texas. And he talked to local farmers and corn growers about the new global agricultural market. You may call this a vacation, but I won't. The president may have wanted to get away, may have wanted to play a little and rest a little, and he did. But it's not all he did.

Mr. Bush is our first MBA president and he has in fact been consciously conducting himself in office as a CEO of a very large business firm. I think his first vacation is a perfect extension of this CEO model—he spent his vacation multitasking!

According to a survey by the American Management Association, CEOs and senior executives may travel far away on vacation, but they're never far from the concerns and problems of the officeplace. "Some 26 percent will be in daily contact with their offices while on vacation, and two-thirds will check in at least once a week. Of these 34 percent remain in touch by e-mail and 52 percent rely on cell phones."[29] As one chief executive officer put it: "You just keep doing what you do, just from a different location. With e-mail, faxes, and cell phones, you'd have to go to the South Pacific Islands to truly get away from your job."[30] Except if you were the president, of course. For sure, he'd still be connected.

Well, maybe the president of the United States and the CEOs of Fortune 1000 firms are bad examples of what we mean by going on vacation. But are there any good examples anymore? Can't people go away and stay disconnected, even for a while? Is the new model for vacationing the Gateway computer ad that features a woman working her laptop while paddling a kayak? Whatever happened to the notion that a well-rested president or _____ (fill in the blank) is a better president or _____ (fill in the blank)? Whatever happened to the once-time-honored ideals of doing "no-thing"while on vacation? Whatever happened to the notion of lounging, loafing, and just plain old recuperating from our labors?

four

Minivacations
THE WEEKEND

**When work is utterly disagreeable and week awaits weekend,
our delight in recreation reveals our misery.**

—*Donald Hall*

A few of us, who are really good or just plain lucky in our
financial and vocational choices, get to take the whole summer
off. Some of us, with sufficient seniority, get a month. Most of
us have the standard—but by no means guaranteed—two
weeks off a year. Many of us make due with the occasional
"four-day-quickie." And a lot of us take our vacations or what
leisure we can find on the weekends—if there is a weekend that
week!

Time off the job, in the form of shorter days, shorter weeks,
more holidays, and longer vacations, has always been a big part
of the union mantra. At the end of the nineteenth century the
major cry and claim of the American labor movement was a
simple and distinct one: *Eight Hours for Work, Eight Hours for Rest, and
Eight Hours for What We Will.* For brief periods in the twentieth
century, for some workers in specific industries, this goal was
actually achieved. But the forty-hour standard week is either a
long-forgotten memory or a still-sought-after dream for most

Americans. As a nation we are working more now than ever before. According to Juliet Schor in her best-selling book, The Overworked American, technological progress and industrialization, rather than resulting in less work, have produced, as her subtitle suggests, more work and the "unexpected decline of leisure."

Research into the history of work shows a surprising array of counterintuitive statistics regarding the amount of time individuals and societies dedicated to work. The lives of so-called primitive peoples, says Schor, are commonly thought to be dominated by the incessant need to work. In fact, primitive or "subsistence peoples" do very little work. For example, says Schor, the Kapauku of Papua never work two days in a row and the Kung Bushman never work longer than six hours a day, two-and-a-half days a week. Australian Aborigines and Sandwich Islanders, when they work, never work more than four hours a day.[1]

The work profiles of the Mediterranean basin and early western Europeans also reflects this pattern of minimal work. Even the industrious and highly productive ancient Egyptians limited work to a total of about seventy days a year, or, on average, once every six days.[2] Nonwork time in ancient Greece and Rome was also plentiful. The Athenians celebrated fifty to sixty annual multiday festivals a year, and in some Greek city-states, such as Tarentum, this figure was more than three times higher. In the old Roman calendar, 109 of 355 days were designated "unlawful for judicial and political business."[3] By the mid–fourth century, the number of public festival days reached 175, which meant that the average Roman worker spent fewer than a third of his or her waking hours at work.[4] (These figures are for freemen and do not reflect the efforts of slave laborers. Clearly, factoring in slave work hours would alter the average working day of free people and slaves alike.)

In medieval times, the Church co-opted and converted many of the old Roman rituals and holidays into Christian holy days and feast days. Between the holy days of Sunday, Christmas, Easter, specific saints' days and feasts, the celebrations of weddings and wakes, and seasonal and political festivals, leisure time in medieval England took up probably one-third of the year. In the *ancien régime* of France there were 180 guaranteed work-free days a year, and in Spain holidays and holy days totaled in excess of five months per year. Throughout all of Europe, it is estimated that, except for harvest time, peasants worked less than twenty hours a week.[5]

As Schor argued, the lives of ordinary people in the Middle Ages or ancient Greece and Rome may not have been easy, pleasant, or particularly abundant, but they were leisurely. Depending upon climate, growing seasons, food supply, caloric intake, social custom, political traditions, and Church edicts, the rhythms and cycles of life and time did not revolve around, nor were they measured by, work. Workers in these societies worked and worked hard, often at backbreaking tasks. But contrary to conventional wisdom, they did not toil from sunup to sundown, 365 days a year. It wasn't until the full flowering of the market system and the industrial revolution in the eighteenth and nineteenth centuries that work took on a Draconian, routinized schedule and began to absorb the vast majority of our waking hours. In the words of the anthropologist Marshall Sahlins, it was the market system that handed down to human beings the sentence of "life at hard labor."[6]

The European and American Industrial Revolution of the eighteenth and nineteenth centuries was undoubtedly the period of the longest and most arduous work schedules in the history of humankind. Although one of the enduring myths of the capitalistic system is that it will reduce human toil and the need to work, this claim did not apply to capitalism in its incubation period. According to Schor, before the eighteenth and nineteenth centuries, labor patterns were seasonal, intermittent, and irregular. But the advent of capitalism immediately resulted in steady employment for fifty-two weeks a year, and seventy-to-eighty-hour six-day workweeks immediately became the norm. If these various figures are correct, at their peak, working hours under capitalism increased between 200 and 300 percent over what they had been in medieval times.[7]

It wasn't until well into the twentieth century, after years of persistent political struggle, that the almost universal policy of "long-hour jobs" (ten-to-sixteen-hour days) and six-day workweeks began to change.[8] Slowly, incrementally, custom, practices, and legislation began to shift to labor's side of the ledger. But the changes produced were neither across-the-board nor long-lasting. As Juliet Schor has suggested, although the forty-hour week was held up as the ideal, its reality was but a short-lived "blip" in the demographics and history of the American workforce.

More Americans than ever are now working more than ever before. As we saw in chapter 1, depending on whose statistics you are willing to accept, 85 percent of Americans average forty-five hours a week on the job and projections suggest that by the year 2010 the average workweek will exceed fifty-eight hours. Whatever the exact numbers, the brute fact remains that nobody, not even the Japanese anymore, seem to be putting more time in on the job than we do.[9] And what has to be kept in mind, of course, is that these figures reflect only hours actually on the job and do not represent the other aspects of our workday such as getting to and from the job, as well as household and family responsibilities.

So much for the union cry of *Eight Hours for Work, Eight Hours for Rest, and Eight Hours for What We Will*. As one pundit put it: "Thank God we invented the weekend. If we hadn't, none of us would have a real life. Because you sure can't call all the hours we put in on the job—a life!"

According to Witold Rybczynski's protracted and eminently readable essay *Waiting For the Weekend*, in a strange and convoluted way we really did culturally create the weekend. In fact, he says, due to historical happenstance, chance, and convenience, we literally created what we now accept as the universal standard of temporal management, the seven-day week.

The weekday-weekend cycle is now an *almost* universal institution in the modern world. Our everyday lives are divided into the rhythmic cadence of five days of work and two days off work. But, says Rybczynski, it has not always been so. He points out that although the seven-day week is now culturally ensconced, it is neither a natural nor a necessarily logical way to calibrate time. A twenty-four-hour day is the duration between one dawn and the next. The month is the amount of time—with some minor adjustments—it takes for the moon to wax, become full, and wane. The year is one full cycle of seasons. "But what," says Rybczynski, "does the week measure? Nothing. At least nothing visible. No natural phenomenon occurs every seven days—nothing happens to the sun, the moon, or the stars. The week is an artificial, man-made interval."[10]

The seven-day week became a definitive part of the Western calendar sometime in the second or third century A.D., in ancient Rome. Before that the Egyptians broke up the month into ten-day periods. The Babylonians had seven-day weeks that were punctuated by one- and two-day miniweeks to compensate for the movement of the moon. The Chinese had a formal cycle of individually named days that added up to sixty-day weeks. And, the Mayan culture had a thirteen-day week to commemorate the Thirteen Gods of the Mayan upper world.[11]

According to Rybczynski, there are a multiplicity of explanations, both practical and magical, to explain why and how the seven-day week became the universal standard. To begin with, he says, there were many "sacred sevens" in the ancient world. There were the "seven wonders of the world," "the seven pillars of wisdom," and the "seven labors of Hercules." Then, of course, there were the "seven Heavenly Wanderers," the planets which the Romans used to name the days of the week: Saturn—

Saturday; the Sun—Sunday; the Moon (which the ancients considered a planet)—Monday; Mars—Tuesday; Mercury—Wednesday; Jupiter—Thursday; and Venus—Friday. Or how about a plausible scientific explanation? Modern biology, suggests Rybczywski, has identified seven natural rhythms of the body—the so-called circaseptan rhythms (heartbeat, blood pressure, oral temperature, acid content of blood, calcium levels, and the amount of cortisol in adrenal glands)—that roughly follow a seven-day cycle of fluctuations. And let's not forget about "Snow White and the Seven Dwarfs," the "Seven Seas," "Seven Brides for Seven Brothers," "7–Up," or "7–Eleven"[12]

Rybczynski argues that whatever the reason or reasons behind the structure and length of the week, we needed some way to cluster days into manageable bunches to better organize our lives, and we simply somehow settled on the number seven.

> [W]hatever else it did, the seven-day cycle provided a convenient structure for the repetitive rhythm of daily activities; not only a day for worship but also a day for baking bread, for washing, for cleaning house, for going to market—and for resting. Surely this over-and-over quality has always been one of the attractions of the week—and of the weekend? "Once a week" is one of the commonest measures of time. The planetary week is not a grand chronometer of celestial movements or a gauge of seasonal changes; it is something both simpler and more profound: a measure of ordinary, everyday life.[13]

Yet, this agreed-upon seven-day cycle did not automatically mean that everyone put in five days a week on the job, and then punch-out time on Friday signaled the beginning of two days of freedom from work. Oh no! The social convention of the workless "week-end" (the grammatically correct spelling of the end-of-the-week, in Italian, fine-settimana, "the end of seven days") awaited the economic surpluses of the Industrial

Revolution, union activism, social and political reforms, and economic necessity.

Although the gradual cutbacks in the length of the work-week were in part a direct response to worker and union demands, the motives of many, if not most, employers were much more self-serving in their nature and purpose. Machines needed to be rested, repaired, and retooled to help guarantee maximum productivity. Shutdowns and shorter working days often had more to do with the needs of the machines and prevailing market conditions than the needs and best interests of the men and women working them. Henry Ford, founder and president of the Ford Motor Company and a staunch antiu-nionist, is a classic example of this less than totally altruistic motivation and principle of action.

In 1914, Ford set into motion a series of prescient innovations which would change the face of industrial production, labor relations, and the purpose and structure of weekends for decades to come. He began applying the general principles of Frederick Winslow Taylor to his Highland Park, Michigan, auto plant by installing a moving conveyer belt. The belt brought the work to the worker and theoretically increased the efficiency and rate of worker productivity. The problem was that initially workers did not respond well to the redundancy, lack of autonomy, and rapid work pace of the conveyor belt system. Consequently, Ford found himself dealing with rising rates of absenteeism, tardiness, and worker turnover. As a corrective he initiated a two-step policy which was designed to indirectly address the well-being of individual workers but was more specifically designed to fulfill the needs and goals of Ford Motor Works.[14]

To begin with, Ford reduced the daily hours in the plant from nine to eight; second, he began to pay his workers five dollars a day.[15] In so doing, he made jobs at Ford more valuable and sought after than in any other plants in the industry, where the going rate was about two dollars a day. If this policy did not exactly breed loyalty, unwavering commitment, and a sense of empowerment (terms not then current in management literature), it did breed feelings of gratitude, a sense of stick-to-itiveness and increased efficiency. In 1926 Ford added yet another carrot to his employees' benefit package when he announced that his factories would be closed all day Saturday.

Though the cumulative effects of Ford's voluntary reforms were praised by the union movement and held up as a model for other industries, Ford's motivation and vision had as much to do with the worker as consumer as with the worker as producer. His rationale was that an increase in pay and leisure would stimulate an increase in consumer spending power which, of course, influenced automobile sales.[16] Like his German colleague, Ferdinand Porsche (inventor of the Volkswagen), Ford set out to produce a "peoples' car"—a car that the average worker, earning an average paycheck, could afford and would have the time to use for weekend outings and pleasure trips. In increasing the pay and the leisure of his own workforce, Ford established the standard he hoped other industries would follow. More than just an inventor, Ford was a shrewd businessman who understood the central ingredient of the laissez-faire economic system: Capitalism requires continuous production and consumption in order to sustain itself. In initiating his supposedly pro-labor policies, Ford was, in effect, priming his own pump.

According to Rybczynski, what finally brought the brief appearance of the eight-hour day and the two-day weekend to offices and factories across America was not altruism, activism, or prosperity. It was, paradoxically, the Great Depression of 1929. The rationale for such a move seemed clear. Shorter hours were seen as a stopgap remedy for unemployment; people would work less, but more people would have jobs. In this manner it was hoped that the capitalistic equilibrium between production and consumption would not be completely thrown out of economic kilter. It wasn't until the New Deal legislation embodied in the Fair Labor Standards Act of 1938 that the law mandated a maximum forty-hour week. But historical necessity intervened again during World War II and wartime production caused the workday to be lengthened to ten hours, including Saturdays and Sundays, if necessary.[17]

At the end of World War II, America entered its "golden years." We were universally recognized as the leader of the Western alliance, the chief military power in the world, and the world's predominant industrial giant. Real opportunity for labor reform was at hand, but rather than being cut back, the pattern of long-hour jobs became part of the fabric of our collective working lives. As a nation, having survived the long lean years of the Depression and the war, we were hungry for the deferred benefits of "normalcy": homes, cars, consumer products and services, gadgets and gizmos of all kinds. Americans had fought in two world wars in the span of twenty-eight years "to save the world for democracy" and wanted to reap the potential fruits of their efforts. And so began the postwar trajectory toward increasing hours on the job in order to acquire money and stuff.

By 1948, the Bureau of Labor Statistics estimated that 13 percent of Americans with full-time jobs worked more than forty-nine hours per week. The forty-hour week quickly became the baseline, rather than the optimum, amount people put in on the job.[18] However, although the length of the workweek in 1949 was not much different from what it had been at the turn of the century, the shape of the week was altered dramatically. After World War II, argued Rybczynski, people were unwilling to work a six- or even five-and-a-half-day week. Although they were willing to put in long hours, they wanted the rhythm of the workweek to be compacted. Thus, the five-day workweek and the two-day weekend became a fixture of American life.[19]

So what do we do with our relatively recently won secular treasure? How do most of us spend our 104 days of weekend time off—more if you count the long holiday weekends such as Labor Day, Memorial Day, and Martin Luther King Day?[20]

Theoretically, the correct answer to what we *should do* with our weekends comes right out of Josef Pieper, G. K. Chesterton, and Thomas Aquinas. Weekends are not simply to reinvigorate us so we can better accomplish our duties as workers! Weekends are not a reward for enduring the undurable! Weekends are not just a break, an intermission, time off between an unending series of projects and tasks!

According to philosophers, pundits, pollsters, and politicians alike, weekends ideally are about freedom. The freedom to let go and let be. The freedom to explore your life, your world, and yourself. The freedom to stop, look, and listen. The freedom to examine an idea, pursue a dream. The freedom to think hard,

to be serious, to ponder great ideas. The freedom to be a dilettante. The freedom to be whimsical, play hard, have fun. The
freedom to be open to newness or nothing at all.

In fact, practically speaking, we spend our weekends in a
variety of different ways depending on who we are, what we
do, where and how we live, and how much we make and can
afford to spend. For most of us, the weekends are usually a
mixed bag of relatively mild and pedestrian activities and expe-
riences.

They usually start with the simple pleasure of sleeping in.
(Which means, if you are over the age of forty, waking up at the
usual workday time but forcing yourself to stay in bed until the
deliciously decadent time of 7:15 A.M.!) Weekends mean being
able to linger over breakfast, coffee, and the paper. They include
a few (if you are lucky) household chores and repairs, as well
as a little shopping. Weekends mean a walk, a run, a workout.
Taking kids to the zoo. Watching a T-ball game. Playing catch in
the backyard. Weekends mean turning off the phone, never getting out of your bathrobe, and watching the Sunday afternoon
NFL doubleheader.

Weekends mean breaking up the patterns of the week.
Weekends are about going out for lunch or dinner, and maybe
taking in a film. In the last twenty years, weekends, especially in
summer and the weekends surrounding Memorial Day and
Christmas, are the prime times that Americans, and increasingly
the world market, go to the movies (see table). Moreover, even
before the couch potato side effect of 9-11-01, more Americans
than ever, according to an account executive at Blockbusters
Video, are "going to the movies at home," with over 55 percent
of their rentals occurring over the weekends.[21]

For a growing portion of the urban middle class there is the
regular, if not weekly, migration to the countryside to visit their
second homes. Summer homes and weekend retreats have
always been a part of the urban experience. They were always a
way for the relatively few and the relatively rich to get away, to

Rank/Name of Movie	Date Opened	Three-Day Box Office (In millions)
1. "Spider-Man"	5/3/02 (Fri.)	$114
2. "Harry Potter and the Sorcerer's Stone"	11/16/01 (Fri.)	$93.5
3. "Star Wars: Episode II Attack of the Clones"	5/17/02 (Fri.)	$86.15
4. "The Lord of the Rings: The Fellowship of the Ring."	12/19/01 (Wed.) (Five days)	$73.1
5. "The Lost World: Jurassic Park"	5/23/97 (Fri.)	$72.1
6. "Planet of the Apes"	7/27/01 (Fri.)	$68.5
7. "The Mummy Returns"	5/4/01 (Fri.)	$68.1
8. "Rush Hour 2"	8/3/01 (Fri.)	$67.4
9. "Star Wars: Episode I The Phantom Menace"	5/19/99 (Wed.) (Five days)	$64.8
10. "Monsters, Inc."	11/2/01 (Fri.)	$62.6
11. "Pearl Harbor"	5/25/01 (Fri.)	$59.1
12. "Hannibal"	2/9/01 (Fri.)	$58
13. "Mission: Impossible 2"	5/24/00 (Wed.) (Five days)	$57.8

avoid the crowds, to take minivacations. Since World War II, the construction and purchase of summer homes have greatly expanded for a number of reasons: better roads and transportation systems; the greater number of cars per household; and, larger household incomes, primarily due to the rise of double-income families. I also believe that the salad days of the Clinton administration allowed a lot of recent "empty nester—boomers" to invest in a second home (as well as more traveling vacations) once the annual drain of college tuition payments was officially over.

Of course, for lots of middle-class singles and couples who don't yet own, or don't want to own, a weekend home, other alternatives are available. According to *USA Today*, from Rhode Island to Fire Island and from the Hamptons to the Jersey Shore, the largely East Coast ritual of hardworking, mostly professional, mostly single adults shedding power suits and pumps for sandals and shorts is in full swing every Friday night. An estimated 25,000 people drive, fly, or entrain to these seaside resorts to spend big money in the pursuit of leisure, pleasure, play, and "beach-house escapism."[22]

Obviously, middle-class couples with children may not have the same options as single people, but they too seek solace on the weekends—hopefully of a more sober kind. Recently a major hotel chain created a national newspaper ad campaign in hopes of capturing this demographic market. The ads read: "Have a family values weekend . . . [A picture of a family playing and having fun together] . . . Your family! Our values! [Weekend rates starting at $59.00]. Join us. Spend time together. Stay connected."[23]

Clearly, not all families or singles have the kinds of weekend options we've been discussing. It's been my experience that weekends in most family households are anything but leisurely or restful. In fact, I would suggest that the management of weekends in most "double-income with some kids households" (DISKS) can best be characterized as an experiment in controlled chaos. Think about it, although you don't have to go into "the job," Saturdays are usually just another workday. A "honey-do list" is drawn up, chores are assigned, and you're both off and running. Take the dog to the vet. Drop off Carla at ballet classes and Jason at little league practice. Pick up the dry cleaning. Stop at the hardware store. Vacuum and dust. Get Carla and Jason, bring them to swimming classes. Go grocery shopping. Pick up kids again. Take Carla to the mall, drop off Jason at the cineplex. Get the dog. Do a load of wash. Start the sauce for dinner. Get the kids. Finish making dinner. Have dinner. Clean up after dinner. Drop off the kids at friends. Pick up two videos "not suitable" for family viewing. Fall asleep halfway through the first one. Totally forget to pick up the kids until they call looking for you.

And then there's Sunday. (You know the routine. Fill in the blanks as you deem necessary.) Church . . . lawn and yardwork . . . Little League game . . . wash the car . . . clean out the garage . . . have dinner with the in-laws . . . check the kids' homework . . . check e-mail for work Monday . . . and—in the words of the late Sonny and the ever-rejuvenate Cher—"the beat goes on."

Pop critics and commentators on the workplace keep telling us that the song that best reflects workers' attitudes about the job is "Thank God It's Friday" sung in celebration of the end of the week. That well may be so, but after a long weekend of kit, kin, and chores, there are a lot of people singing a slightly different tune—"Thank God It's Monday!"—in celebration of the end, finally, of the weekend!

Witold Rybczynski ends *Waiting For the Weekend* with a warning:

> [T]he weekend has imposed a rigid schedule on our free time, which can result in a sense of urgency ("soon it will be Monday") that is at odds with relaxation. The weekly rush to the cottage is hardly leisurely, nor is the compression of various

recreational activities into the two-day break. The freedom to do something has become the obligation to do something . . . [24]

The weekend has become "the chief temporal institution of the modern age."[25] We invented the weekend as a retreat and refuge from labor. We created it to find leisure and thereby overcome the alienation, meaninglessness, and ennui of work. Think about it. Few of us regularly ask each other, "How was your (work)week?" But the salutation and interrogative, "How was your weekend?" is common.

Weekends, Rybczynski suggests, are in danger of becoming their own antithesis. He points out that we have become determined and frenetic in the pursuit of weekend pleasures, both large and small. We try too hard to make up for the "pain and emptiness" of the week by doing things and staying busy all weekend long. According to Rybczynski, the protocols and rituals of the weekends "represent an enslavement of a kind." At best, they are a "deceptive placebo" to counteract the boredom and exhaustion of the workplace.[26]

For too many of us, concludes Rybczynski, weekends represent a different and sometimes a more pleasant way of staying busy and consuming time. But, he says, genuine free time, real leisure, must remain just that: "Free of the encumbrance of convention, free of the need for busyness, free for the 'noble habit of doing nothing.'"[27] And clearly, "doing nothing" does not describe the modern weekend!

five

Shopping as Leisure and Play

The idea of more, of ever increasing wealth, has become the center of our identity and our security, and we are caught by it as an addict by his drugs.

—Paul Wachtel

Whether for a week, weeks at a time, or just a weekend, millions of Americans go on vacation each year. Millions and millions more, however, out of choice or necessity, don't. So, the question becomes—for those who do not travel, do not take a vacation—how do they recreate? What do they do for leisure? How do they play?

According to the Harvard economist Juliet Schor, although lots of Americans seek solace in hobbies, in volunteer organizations, in the contemplative solitude of a book, or in the aesthetics and anesthetic effects of television, most of us seek comfort and consolation in the pleasures and products of shopping. In her disturbingly accurate book *The Overspent American*, Schor argues that we are both children and captives of a "culture of consumerism." For far too many of us, "shopping till we drop" is not just a satirical cliché but, rather, an honorific—a lifestyle to be wished for and sought after.[1]

In America, Schor argues, shopping has become a "primary pleasure principle," a "birthright," and our most common form of "psychological release" and "stress reduction." It has been transmogrified from a "basic necessity," to a "form of recreation," to a "lifestyle." For more and more of us, the activities and rituals of shopping have become our main means of recreation and diversion. It is the vehicle that more and more of us use to *vacate* ourselves from our workaday lives.

In his fascinating book *The Day Before Yesterday: Reconsidering America's Past, Rediscovering the Future*, the journalist and political commentator Michael Elliot suggests that the birth of our "modern culture of consumerism" coincides with the end of World War II. In 1945, says Elliot, based on the "twin rocks of its economic and military might," America "bestrode the . . . world like a colossus."[2] Not only had we militarily defeated the Axis powers in the field, but we had also produced the necessary military hardware, both for ourselves and our Allies, to do so. After the war the issue became: could we reconvert to a peacetime economy? Could we beat and bend our bullets back into plowshares? Clearly, the answer was yes. By 1946, the United States accounted for more than 40 percent of the world's total economic output, higher than any nation before. Cars were once again rolling off assembly lines that had been producing tanks, household goods were back on the shelves at Sears and Montgomery Ward, rationing was over, and universities were jammed with ex-GIs eager to better themselves. The general economy was in high gear. It was no longer "the worst of times"; it was we were righteously convinced— "the best of times." We embraced the "golden years," says Elliot, as the fruition of the "American Dream." We had survived the Depression, won the war, and had officially become a "people of plenty." As one commentator described America's attitude in the 1950s: "The War is over. Let's make babies and build houses and get down to business."[3] The postwar boom economy was a benchmark we sought to maintain, expand, and pass on to future generations.[4]

On the basis of Schor's calculations, the level of production in America since 1948 has more than doubled. What this means is that we can now produce enough goods and services to live at our 1948 standard of living (measured in market-available services and goods) in less than half the time it took in 1948. This in turn means that if we chose to, we could work four hours a day; or work a year in six months; or every worker in America could take every other year off with pay. Just do the arithmetic, says Schor. So why—given our poverty of time and the burdens of work—haven't we traded our prosperity for leisure?[5] "Why," asks Schor, "has leisure been such a conspicuous casualty of prosperity?" Or, as Daniel Bell put it, what keeps the American worker, "like the mythical figure of Ixion," chained seemingly forever to the endless revolving wheel of work?[6] The answer, of course, is obvious. In biblical terms, it's called "things of the flesh." In economic terms, it is called the "immediate gratification of consumer goods"—a house, a car, appliances, gadgets, whatnots, and all manner of other creature comforts.

Free-market capitalism and its fruits (consumer products and services), says the economist William Grieder, is the secular religion of our time.[7] Simply put, we have become addicted to the fruits of our production. We have traded our time and remain chained to our jobs in order to obtain consumer products and services. We have deconstructed Aristotle's adage "the purpose of work is the attainment of leisure" to the far baser notion "I work in order to consume and possess." We have become a society of "conspicuous consumers" where wants equal needs, and needs clamor for instant fulfillment and gratification.

In his now classic antiestablishment text, *One Dimensional Man*, Herbert Marcuse points out that we have made a tautology out of the equation: The goods of life are equal to the good life. Marcuse contends that as a society, we are infatuated with the benefits of science, technology, and industrialism because they have been able to produce a lifestyle to which we have become both accustomed and addicted. In most industrial countries, modern-day capitalism, suggests Marcuse, has fulfilled an age-old dream of humankind: freedom from basic want. No matter what the political limits and drawbacks, the system has proved to be efficient in its capacity to produce a seemingly unlimited number and variety of products and services. We have been numbed by the niceties of the system, suggests Marcuse. People find comfort and recognize themselves in their commodities. They find their soul in their auto, their status and identity in their stereo system, their home, their wardrobe.[8]

In a lesser-known but equally antiestablishment text, *To Have or To Be?*, Erich Fromm contends that the ruling philosophy of our day is not "to be much" but "to have much." We are caught, he says, in a consumer society in which individuals are known both by their professions and by their power over and in the marketplace. The difference between "being" and "having," says Fromm, is not simply an empty metaphysical notion. It is, rather, the key difference between a society centered around persons and one centered around things. The "having" orientation is characteristic of Western industrial society, in which greed for money, fame, and power has become the dominant theme of life. Fromm argues that in modern society "citizen" and "consumer" are synonymous terms, and all consumers identify themselves by the formula: "I am what I have and what I consume."[9]

Consumerism assumes that having more is being more and if some is good, more must absolutely be better. It identifies well-being with buying, accumulating, and displaying consumer goods and services. Consumerism is perceived as an acquired right and a national characteristic. Though we poke fun at our materialistic obsessiveness—"He who has the most toys, wins!"; "Nothing succeeds like excess!"; "So many malls, and so little trunk space!"—we do not renounce it.[10] Instead of disparaging the tendency to want more than we need, we have elevated it to the status of a private duty and a public virtue. We are, seemingly, in complete accord with Adam Smith's dictum: "Consumption is the sole end and purpose of all production."[11] Wanting more is neither excessive nor a vice in a consumer society. To shop is not merely to pass time or simply to acquire goods and services. To shop is to be!

Juliet Schor claims that we live in the most consumer-oriented society in history. The average American is consuming more than twice as much as he or she did forty years ago. This holds true, she says, not only for the higher-end Gucci set but all the way down the income scale. Every stratum of worker has participated in the postwar consumption boom. Today, on average, Americans spend three to four times as many hours per year shopping as do their counterparts in Western European countries. Shopping has literally become a leisure activity in its own right. Going to the mall (malling) and hanging out a the mall (mallratting) is a common Friday or Saturday night's entertainment not only for teenagers, who seem to live and breed there, but for adults as well. Seventy percent of the American population visit malls at least once a week. This is a greater percentage of the population than those who attend church on a regular but not a weekly basis. Shopping has become the most popular form of family weekday-evening out-of-home entertainment.[12]

The simple fact, says Schor, is that outside of watching television, shopping is the chief cultural activity in the United States. On average, adults shop in excess of six hours a week for both necessary and luxury products and services.[13] Again, on average, Americans spend nearly seven times as much time shopping as they do playing with their kids.[14] And, finally, according to Anna Quindlen, Americans spend more time shopping than reading.[15]

Americans used to travel to see the sights and meet people. Regretfully, said Schor, that is no longer the case. Born-to-shop guide books are rapidly outselling and replacing Fodor and

"Developer on Holiday" by Horsey. © 1990 Seattle Post-Intelligencer Tribune Media Services. Used with permission.

Baedeker. (Recently a new shopping magazine has been launched to help. Consumers find that "perfect little something" that they "just gotta have!" It's called Lucky—available on the Web at www.luckymag.com.) Once a purely utilitarian chore, Schor points out, shopping in America has been elevated to the status of an obsession.[16] As one woman put it, "[I realized] I was a compulsive shopper when it dawned on me that I knew all of the UPS drivers in my neighborhood. They all waved and said hello by my first name!"[17]

Malls are now everywhere and growing by the moment. By 1987, there were more shopping malls in America than high schools.[18] Over one billion square feet of our total land area has been converted into shopping centers. That's about sixteen square feet of mall space for every man, woman, and child in America.[19] Bloomington, Minnesota, is the home of Mall of

America. MOA, as the locals call it, is the largest enclosed shopping and entertainment complex in the U.S. with 4.2 million square feet of shopping space and "where it's always 72 degrees." It has more than 400 stores, a theme park, two food courts, a 1.2-million-gallon aquarium, arcades, mini-golf courses, a chapel where couples can get married, and a fourteen-screen movie theater. An MOA brochure claims it's big enough to hold a total of thirty-two 747 airplanes or seven Yankee Stadiums. MOA also claims to attract more visitors annually than does the Grand Canyon and Disney World combined.[20]

With the continuous sprawling of suburbia, malls have become our substitutes for "local neighborhood shopping centers." Whether intended or not, malls, big and small, have radically affected the well-being and fundamental viability of large urban downtown areas as well as the main streets of small-town America. Inner-city downtown and neighborhood shopping areas are generally losing the battle with the satellite suburban malls, and prosperous "Main Streets" now only exit in the prose of Sherwood Anderson and the radio stories of Garrison Keillor. Malls have become the "centers of many communities," says Michael Jacobsen of the Center for the Study of Commercialism. "They are a natural destination to fill a bored life" for young and old alike. Malls are the "new downtowns," the new "stores on the corner." They are where we go to meet, eat, shop, and see a show.

Besides changing the locales of where we shop, the "malling of America" has changed the kinds of stores we shop at. The days of a few major department stores and a battery of boutique shops are now ancient history. The "malling of America" directly coincides with the "franchising of America" or the "chaining of America."

The "chaining of America" has happened so quickly that it's hard to believe the statistics. In 1972, independent booksellers claimed 58 percent of all book sales. By 1997 their share had fallen to just 17 percent, and it continues to fall. Lowe's and Home Depot control more than a quarter of the hardware market . . . There are similar statistics for pharmacies, 11,000 of which have recently disappeared, as well as video stores, coffee shops, and office supply stores. Overall, more than half a million franchise businesses in 60 different industries control 35 percent of the retail market.[21]

Putting architectural style and location aside, most new malls wind up having the same feel and ambience. From the MOA in Minnesota to Gurnee Mills in Illinois to the Galleria in Houston, Texas—they all seem and feel strikingly similar because they all contain the same kinds of stores, the same types of products, and, more often than not, the same national chains and franchises. (Question: Is there a mall in America that *doesn't* have a McDonald's and a Starbucks?) What results is boringly obvious: most of us shop the same stores, buy the same kinds of products, and wind up at least looking and sometimes behaving much too much alike. Sloan Wilson's *The Man in the Gray Flannel Suit* (1955) is back, and all of his grandchildren are wearing jeans from The Gap, shirts from Banana Republic, hats from Eddie Bauer, and shoes from Foot Locker. In the words of James Kuwtsher, author of *The Geography of Nowhere*, "Everyplace looks like no place and no place looks like home."

Of course, nowadays you don't even have to leave your home or get out of your favorite armchair in order to be guilty of "conspicuous consumption." Phone lines and mail boxes are direct conduits to thousands of potential products. Most homes, says Juliet Schor, are now virtual retail outlets, with cable shopping channels, mail-order catalogs, toll-free numbers, and computer hookups. In 2000, some 40 billion mail-order catalogs flooded our homes, which works out to be about 150 catalogs for each one of us.[22] And, in 1996, 53 percent of all Americans bought something by phone or mail.[23] It is now estimated that 20 percent of us are online at least five hours a week, and most of that time we're shopping. Although Internet transactions are still relatively small compared with "brick and mortar" business receipts, the numbers keep growing. According to E-marketer's "E-commerce: B2C Report," consumers spent $30.1 billion online in 1999 and $59.7 billion online in 2000. In 2001, NPR and newspaper sources reported a more modest rate of e-sales of $44.5 billion, with projections of $144 billion in sales by 2006.[24]

Whether by catalog, via e-mail, or at the malls, according to the National Retail Foundation, in 1999 Americans spent nearly $200 billion on holiday gifts, or $850 per consumer. As a nation we now annually spend $6 trillion a year mostly on consumer goods, which averages out to $21,000 per person.[25] Now, it may not be true that we are all guilty of "shopping until we drop," and it may not even be true that we all "love to shop." But we all "shop a lot," and clearly we live in a "culture of consumption."

Arthur Miller, in his seldom-staged play, *The Price* (1968), dramatically spells out at least part of the reason for our obsession with shopping. The play is set in the attic of a Manhattan brownstone. Two middle-aged brothers have met there to sell their dead father's effects. They have called in a used furniture dealer named Soloman to sell everything off. The attic is crammed with ten rooms of furniture. There are armchairs, couches, settees, bureaus, armoires, and desks. All of the furniture is sturdy and substantial, and although it is old, it is clean and in usable condition. The brothers expect to make a substantial amount from the sale and are somewhat put off and angry when the dealer offers them a price well below what they were expecting. They accuse the dealer of trying to cheat them. They argue that the furniture is in good shape and built to last forever. That, says Soloman, is the point. It's too good! It's too solid! It's never going to break! Nobody, he says, is going to want it. What people really want, says Soloman, is disposable. Nowadays, he says, everything has got to be disposable—the car, the wife, the kids. The point is, when you're tired of it, don't want it anymore, throw it away, go shopping, buy a new one. In fact, he says, he's taking a risk buying it from them. He lectures to them on the nuances of shopping, quality, and cash value in a thick Yiddish accent.

> . . . Because you see main thing today is—shopping. Years ago a person, he was unhappy, didn't know what to do with him-self—he'd go to church, start a revolution—*something*. Today, you're unhappy? Can't figure it out? What is the salvation? Go shopping. . . .

He goes on to say:

> . . . I'm telling you the truth! If they would close the stores for six months in this country there would be from coast to coast a regular massacre. With this kind of furniture the shopping is over, it's finished, there's no more possibilities, you got it, you see? So you got a problem here.[26]

Within our "culture of consumption" the specific reason(s) why individuals shop, spend, and buy are many, varied, and, more often than not, interconnected. We consume out of need, desire, joy, whim, fancy, or pleasure. We consume to acquire and estab-lish personal identity; to establish pedigree and a place in the pecking order; to get up to the Joneses; to keep up with the Joneses; and, if we are lucky, to outdo the Joneses! We busy our-selves with shopping to demonstrate skill, talent, and taste; to ful-fill the expectations of others; to mask inadequacies and flaws; to overcome boredom; and, to mask unhappiness. We consume as an antidote to stress and despair, and to compensate for whatever is missing in our lives. But whatever our reasons for our various prize purchases, the bottom line is the same for everybody. What we buy speaks volumes about who and what we are. Because, like it or not, in this society we "communicate with commodities."[27]

The mechanism that drives and directs our "fetishism with commodities" and "culture of consumption" is, to no one's surprise, the seductive siren call of the "cult of advertisement." As marketing scholar William Lazar wrote in the 1960s, "It is impossible to understand fully the American culture without a comprehension of advertisement."[28] The ad industry, said Lazar, is not just in the business of giving people what they want or need or to simply fulfill their "natural inclinations." The role and goal of advertisement, said Lazar, in an age of automation and plenty is to overcome the limits of our "natural inclinations" and to stimulate interest in and the purchase of new products and services. For Lazar, "continued economic growth" in a mass-production industrial economy requires a society committed to mass consumption. It is therefore part of marketing's calling, said Lazar, to stimulate the desire for consumer wants and needs and to help develop new consumption standards which encourage self-indulgence, luxury, and nonutilitarian products and options.[29]

The culture historian Christopher Lasch has argued that modern advertising seeks to promote self-doubt as much as self-indulgence. That is, through slogans, catchwords, jingles, mottoes, and images, the intrusion of advertisement makes us aware of what we don't have. Advertisement makes us feel incomplete and inadequate, says Lasch, and then proposes consumption as the only cure.[30] Michael Jacobson and Laurie Mazur, in their important book Marketing Madness, agree that the paradoxical goal of advertisement is to create both discontent and desire. Ads simultaneously say and ask: *Do you have one of these? Why not? Everyone has one! Aren't they nice? Don't you want one too? Why be different? Why do without? Why be miserable? Why be left behind? Be somebody! Get one! Tell a friend too!*[31]

> A thousand times a day, in a million forms, calling to us from billboards, magazines, television, radio, newspapers, movies, Web sites, and telemarketers, every single message without exception is this: You are not enough. You do not have enough. You are not happy. You have not achieved the American Dream. . . . Until and unless you buy what we are selling, *you*

will never be happy. . . . If you ever want to be that happy, you had better buy from us while you have the chance.[32]

Paradoxically, suggest Jacobsen and Mazur, the goal of advertisement is to encourage us to meet and achieve our non-material needs through material ends. The message of the "adcult industry" is straightforward and at the same time, mystic and metaphysical: *You can buy happiness. You can be loved. You can be accepted. You can be transformed into the person you want to be. Just get our product, and keep buying our product until we come up with another product you will want and need.* This message, say the authors, is repeated in every media, "twenty-four/seven" from cradle to grave.

The average American will spend nearly two years of his or her life watching TV commercials. The average half-hour TV show now has eight minutes of commercials. Today's children are exposed to up to 2,000 commercials a day. Two-thirds of the space in our newspapers is devoted to advertisement. Nearly half of the mail we receive is selling something. Most of us see, hear, or read approximately 2,400 words of ad copy a week. The outdoor advertising industry is a $5 billion-a-year business with more than a billion spent on billboards. Because of all this and more, it is estimated that by the age of twenty, Americans have been exposed to over one million commercial messages.[33]

The importance of the role that advertisement plays in our society, for good or ill, can perhaps be illustrated by a brief look at the money we spend on the enterprise. According to *Advertising Age* in 2001 the total tab spent on advertisements of all kinds was $231,287,000,000. The breakdown by medium and location looks something like this.[34]

Newspaper	$17,729,000,000
National	2,932,000,000
Local	14,797,000,000
Magazine	16,417,000,000

Sunday Magazine	1,157,000,000

Television
Network TV	18,638,000,000
Spot TV	14,100,000,000
Syndicated TV	3,192,000,000
Cable TV Networks	10,291,000,000

Radio
Network	834,000,000
Spot (National)	2,164,000,000

Outdoor	2,380,000,000

Internet	5,752,000,000

Yellow Pages	13,592,000,000

Again, according to the *Advertising Age*, the following is a list of the ten top big spenders in advertising in 2001.

1. General Motors $3,374,400,000
2. Procter & Gamble   2,540,600,000
3. Ford Motor Co.   2,408,200,000
4   Pepsi Co.   2,210,400,000
5. Pfizer   2,189,500,000
6. Daimler Chrysler   1,985,300,000
7. AOL Time Warner   1,885,300,000
8. Philip Morris Cos.   1,815,700,000
9. Walt Disney Co.   1,757,300,000
10. Johnson & Johnson   1,618,100,000

To say the least, that's a hell-of-a-lot of money being spent on essentially the same simple message: "Want, desire, consume!" Or, to give the adcult industry's message its proper due:

Wanna be somebody? Wanna forget all your cares and woes? Wanna have fun? Go shopping and buy something!

In 1917, America and the world experienced the first influenza epidemic, which struck down and killed an estimated 20 million victims. Today, we are all suffering from a pandemic of *affluenza* (noun: "a painful, contagious, socially transmitted condition of overload, debt, anxiety, and waste resulting from the dogged pursuit of more"). And, at the moment, say John DeGraaf, David Wann, and Thomas Naylor, authors of the book and PBS special *Affluenza: The All-Consuming Epidemic*, there is no known cure or immunization for this malady. All of us, they warn, are at some risk of "shopping ourselves to death."

The affluenza epidemic, claim the authors, is rooted in the obsessive, almost religious quest for economic expansion that has become the core principle of what is called the "American dream."[35] "Our civilization," wrote Al Gore, the man-who-would-be-president, in his days as a senator and an environmentalist, "promises happiness through the consumption of an endless stream of shiny new products . . . But the promise is always false."[36] We constantly pursue more in the hope of finding meaning, purpose, love, satisfaction, and/or pleasure. But, at best, what most us find is a *Sale!* Nevertheless, as one shopper confided: "It's easier to buy something new and feel good about yourself than it is to change yourself or deal with reality."[37] Going shopping, buying stuff, acquiring possessions is a quick and immediate response to the tedium of work and everyday living. In lieu of other forms of meaningful activity, shopping can be seen as a creative outlet, a playful event, or, at the very least, a non-job-related experience and a temporary escape from the day-to-day world.

Karl Marx once suggested that religion is the opiate of the people. The Chicago playwright Belinda Bremner now claims that shopping may be the new opiate of the people, or maybe even the new religion of the people, because "shopping can produce a state of anesthetized transcendence."

And on Sunday, the end of the endless work week, we worship at the shrine of the holy half-price. We rejoice and are exceedingly glad in the bargain and the deal and the promise of a perfect life if we just buy this one more _____ (fill in the blank!). We have traded scapulars and tallithes for new badges of faith—designer logos and labels. No longer afraid to utter the name of the Almighty, we wear it writ-large on every item. We purge our pain when we splurge our gain. Ritual cleansing shopping! Shop Therapy! Baptism by fire sale! Next year in the Mall of America—we long to go on a pilgrimage of purchase. We make the stations and try on the mysteries. All the while believing that if we but search hard enough—the peace that passeth all under-standing can be found at 40 to 70 percent off![38]

Now let's be honest with ourselves. We love to shop, we want to shop, and, at a very basic level, we need to shop and consume. The desire to consume is not wrong. Critics of the consumer economy are not attacking *every pleasure* that can be associated with the acquisition of products or services that we need, want, or just flat out desire. We need *stuff*. Economic systems are created to produce the *stuff* we need. Even superfluous *stuff*, trivial *stuff*, luxurious *stuff* is not necessarily wrong, decadent, or bourgeois. This issue is not consumerism per se, but shopping as an addiction, a fetish, a diversion, an obsession, a metaphysical orientation toward life. Shopping as a substitute for living.

The nationally syndicated comic strip *Cathy* by Cathy Guisewite specializes in satirizing "yuppie" and middle-class lifestyles and consumer patterns. In the late 1980s, Guisewite did a Sunday story line that perfectly captures the spirit of "commodity fetishism" or "product idolatry." In each frame of the cartoon are two characters surrounded by a sea of high-end consumer goods. He says, displaying and describing each item in turn: "An anodized aluminum multi-lens three-beam mini-excavation spotlight that will live its life in the junk drawer with dead batteries. A professional designer's magnifying draft lamp that will never be in a room with an idea." She says, holding up her goodies for all to see: "An industrial stainless steel pasta vat that will never see a noodle or a group." He says: "Architectural magazines we don't read. . . . " She says: "A 10-function answering machine with anti-tap device for a telephone that never rings . . . " He says: "A deep sea dive watch that will never get damp." She says: "Keys to a four-wheel drive vehicle that will never experience a hill. . . . " And in the final frame, he announces: "Abstract materialism has arrived." "Yes," she sadly concurs, "we've moved past things that we want and need and are buying those things that have nothing to do with our lives!"[39] As William A. McDonough, dean of the School of Architecture at the University of Virginia, put the question: "When did we stop being people with lives, to become consumers with lifestyles?"[40]

The former Czech president and playwright Vaclav Havel warns us of the spiritual and moral disease engendered by a consumer culture. Shopping, he says, is a "desperate substitute for living." When life "becomes reduced to a hunt for consumer goods, freedom becomes trivialized to mean "a chance to freely choose which washing machine or refrigerator we want to buy." Consumer bliss, Havel points out, diverts people's attention from the community to the self. A consumer culture makes it easy to accept the slow erosion of social, political, and moral standards because their passing is hardly noticed—we're all too busy shopping![41]

Okay, let's have some semiserious fun!. Where are you on the leisure shopping spectrum? Are you a shopaholic? Are you a consumaholic? Are you suffering from affluenza? In the privacy of your own home, without anyone looking over your shoulder, take the following diagnostic quiz to see if you have affluenza or are susceptible to it. If you have it, believe me you're not alone! If you don't have it—bravo! Keep it up and tell others about the secret to your success!

Affluenza Self-Diagnosis Test

Yes No

☐ ☐   1. Do you get bored unless you have something to con-
        sume (goods, food, media)?

☐ ☐   2. Do you try to impress your friends with what you
        own, or where you vacation?

☐ ☐   3. Do you ever use shopping as "therapy"?

☐ ☐   4. Do you sometimes go to the mall just to look around,
        with nothing specific to buy?

☐ ☐   5. Do you buy home improvement products in a large
        chain store rather than the neighborhood hardware
        store?

☐ ☐   6. Have you ever gone on a vacation primarily to shop?

☐ ☐   7. In general, do you think about things more than you
        think about people?

☐ ☐   8. When you pay utility bills, do you ignore the amount
        of resource consumed?

☐ ☐   9. Given the choice between a slight pay raise and a
        shorter workweek, would you choose the money?

☐ ☐   10. Do you personally fill more than one large trash bag in
        a single week?

☐ ☐   11. Have you ever lied to a family member about the
        amount you spent for a product?

☐ ☐   12. Do you frequently argue with family members about
        money?

☐ ☐   13. Do you volunteer your time less than five hours a week
        to help other people?

☐ ☐ 14. Do you routinely compare the appearance of your lawn and/or home with others in your neighborhood?

☐ ☐ 15. Does each person in your house or apartment occupy more than 500 square feet of personal space?

☐ ☐ 16. Do you routinely gamble or buy lottery tickets?

☐ ☐ 17. Do you check your investments at least once a day?

☐ ☐ 18. Are any of your credit cards "maxed out"?

☐ ☐ 19. Do worries about debt cause you physical symptoms like headaches or indigestion?

☐ ☐ 20. Do you spend more time shopping every week than you do with your family?

☐ ☐ 21. Do you frequently think about changing jobs?

☐ ☐ 22. Have you had cosmetic surgery to improve your appearance?

☐ ☐ 23. Do your conversations often gravitate toward things you want to buy?

☐ ☐ 24. Are you sometimes ashamed about how much money you spend on fast food?

☐ ☐ 25. Do you sometimes weave back and forth in traffic to get somewhere faster?

☐ ☐ 26. Have you ever experienced road rage?

☐ ☐ 27. Do you feel like you're always in a hurry?

☐ ☐ 28. Do you often throw away recyclable materials rather than take the time to recycle them?

☐ ☐ 29. Do you spend less than an hour a day outside?

☐ ☐ 30. Are you *unable* to identify more than three wildflowers that are native to your area?

☐ ☐   31. Do you replace sports equipment before it's worn out to have the latest styles?

☐ ☐   32. Does each member of your family have his or her own TV?

☐ ☐   33. Is the price of a product more important to you than how well it was made?

☐ ☐   34. Has one of your credit cards ever been rejected by a salesperson because you were over the limit?

☐ ☐   35. Do you receive more than five mail-order catalogs a week?

☐ ☐   36. Are you one of those consumers who almost never takes a reusable bag to the grocery store?

☐ ☐   37. Do you ignore the miles per gallon of gasoline your car gets?

☐ ☐   38. Did you choose the most recent car you bought partly because it enhanced your self image?

☐ ☐   39. Do you have more than five active credit cards?

☐ ☐   40. When you get a raise at work, do you immediately think about how you can spend it?

☐ ☐   41. Do you drink more soft drink, by volume, than tap water?

☐ ☐   42. Did you work more this year than last year?

☐ ☐   43. Do you have doubts that you'll be able to reach your financial goals?

☐ ☐   44. Do you feel "used-up" at the end of your workday?

☐ ☐   45. Do you usually make just the minimum payment on credit card bills?

☐ ☐ 46. When you shop, do you often feel a rush of euphoria followed by anxiety?

☐ ☐ 47. Do you sometimes feel like your personal expenses are so demanding that you can't afford public expenses like schools, parks, and transit?

☐ ☐ 48. Do you have more stuff than you can store in your house?

☐ ☐ 49. Do you watch TV more than 2 hours a day?

☐ ☐ 50. Do you eat meat nearly every day?

Scoring your Results

Each "yes" answer carries a weight of two points. If you're uncertain as to your answer, or it's too close to call, give yourself one point. If you score:

0–25   You have no serious signs of affluenza.
25–50   You are mildly infected.
50–7   Your temperature is rising quickly. You've got a problem.
75–100 You've got affluenza big time! See the doctor, and take appropriate actions immediately. You may be contagious. There's no time to lose!

Source: John de Graaf, David Wann, and Thomas H. Naylor, *Affluenza: The All-Consuming Epidemic* (San Francisco: Berrett-Koehler Publishers, Inc., 2001). Reprinted with permission.

six

Sports
and Play

The true amateur athlete . . . is one who takes up sport for the
fun and love of it, and to whom success or defeat is a secondary
matter so long as the play is good . . . It is from doing the thing
well, doing the thing handsomely, doing the thing intelligently
that one derives the pleasure which is the essence of sport."

—William James

So far, we have talked about leisure and culture, vacations and
traveling, time off around the house, and weekends away. We've
also talked about shopping as a form of play and a psychological substitute for leisure. Yet another access to play and a quick
fix for leisure is to seek diversion, recreation, and renewal in the
Wide World of Sports.

In the nineteenth century, there was a rather famous English
phrase: "Gin (drink) is the quickest way out of Manchester." At
the time, Manchester was England's leading center of coal min-
ing and production. Mines in those days were deep, dark, dan-
gerous holes in the ground. The miners worked long hours,
under horrible conditions, for bad pay. Once their shift in the
dark was over, getting drunk to get over the horrors of the day
and to get up enough courage to go back again in the morning

seemed a reasonable thing to do. Gin was simply the handiest and cheapest way to escape the tedium and dangers of a depressing job and lifestyle. Today in America, it can be argued that the quickest way to relax, unwind, and get over the job remains, in part, "drink" (but beer now more than gin) and "sports." To be exact, the preferred "drug of choice" is really some combination of "drink and sports."

To be a sports fan, at any and every level, and in regard to literally any contest, activity, event, or game we call a sport (e.g., team tiddlely winks or Olympic curling) is to achieve instant escape, gratification, and pleasure. According to the sports scholar Christian Messenger, "sportsworld is the American environment."[1] In the past five decades we have turned to sports more than any other popular cultural activity for release and relaxation. Sports at every level, professional or amateur, is how more and more of us, as spectators or participants, spend our time, money, energy, and attention. And because of our collective exposure, the aesthetics of sports more and more affects our understanding of what is valuable, beautiful, remarkable, and fun in our lives. The spectacle of sports now creates the metaphors by which many of us classify and understand the world, ourselves, and others. It establishes the meter for measurement and merit. And at the very least, or perhaps most important, the spectacle of sports anesthetizes us to that which we are either unable or unwilling to deal with in our own lives. What is more, there is a bonus prize connected to all of this. If you are a moderate tippler of your drink of choice, you will be able to achieve this magical moment of metaphysical brainwashing without the penalty of a painful and prolonged physical hangover!

Before I proceed, a point of clarification is required. In making the claim that we are a society that is addicted to sports, I mean men and women alike and for that matter children and young adults as well. In making this claim, I am fully aware that the four major sports (baseball, football, basketball, and

Tennis Match. © Corel.

hockey) are primarily watched by a male audience and that the listenership of sports talk radio is 95 percent male. (The media and the advertising community are aware of these facts as well. They reportedly spend millions each year trying to entice a larger female audience.) It is, of course, not the case that women don't watch the "big four pro sports." They do. But they primarily watch other kinds of sports, skill sports such as tennis, finesse sports such as golf, and special sporting events, such as the Olympics. The language of sports may not trip off the tongue of most women, but a majority of them can at least carry on a basic conversation.

Part of the reason women watch less sports and different kinds of sports is tied up in the intricacies of the "politics of gender." Mariah Burton Nelson, athlete and author, has written a brilliant and blistering book on sexism and the culture of sports titled *The Stronger Women Get, the More Men Love Football*. Nelson believes that the more power women have acquired—athletically, economically, and politically—the more threatened men feel, and the more they cling to football and other manly sports as a reaction to and a buffer against feminism. The manly sports—the "big four" plus boxing and wrestling—are the only areas where male muscle matters. It's a testosterone-induced high, a very exclusive men's club. Men may have to deal with assertive wives and daughters and take a back seat to a female boss, but football remains the last bastion of mythical male domination. So, says Nelson, when women claim they can compete with men on an equal basis almost anywhere, men reply: "Thank God for football!"

As part of this dynamic, Nelson suggests that women consciously and unconsciously turn away from these sports and leave the men to their clannish celebration of manliness. At the same time, says Nelson, many women resent "the time their husbands, fathers, or brothers spend screaming at the tube, slapping raucous high-fives, and indulging in loud emotional outbursts that seem misplaced and out of proportion to the drama at hand."[2] Men, of course, see Nelson's book as a radical feminist tract, an attempt to invade a sacred male sanctuary. Most of the women I've talked to, on the other hand, see it is a moderate, clearly argued, commonsensical and objective analysis of our society's (and especially men's) preoccupation with sports.

To put all this aside, the fact of the matter is that sports are part of the fabric of our social calendars and private lives. Holidays have long been dominated by sports scheduling. For over thirty-five years, most Thanksgiving dinners have been planned around the Detroit Lions football game (11 A.M. CST) and the Dallas Cowboys game (5:30 P.M. CST). Christmas night usually has a marquee NBA game in the early evening, so families can wind down after a long day of food and presents and being "forced to spend time together." The activities on New Year's Eve and New Year's Day are, of course, driven by the timing of the various college bowl games. And as we have all come to know and accept, the beginning of spring is the start of the baseball season and fall is ushered in by the first game of the World Series. (By the way, there are only two days a year when *no professional games* of any kind are played: the day before and the day after the baseball All-Star Game.)

Besides being glued to the tube or being part of the crowd in the stands, participating in sports for fun and fitness is also a regular part of the lives of many Americans. In a recent survey literally millions of men and women reported, if not bragged, that they regularly participated in sporting and workout events: exercise walking, 77.6 million; swimming, 58.2 million; exercising with equipment, 46.1 million; bicycle riding, 43.5 million; golf, 27.5 million; hiking, 27.5 million; roller skating, 27.0 million; running/jogging, 22.5 million; volleyball, 14.8 million; calisthenics, 11.8 million; step aerobics, 8.5 million; and, handball, 2.2 million. [3]

So, like it or not, sports are part of who we are as individuals and a society. For some they are a form of release, recreation, and relaxation. For others, they can become an addiction, a form of escapism, and an obsession.

The nineteenth-century German philosopher G. W. F. Hegel said that you can understand and measure a people and a society by the gods they worship. In this society, one of our gods, one of our major icons, is sports of all kinds. According to the media maven Neil Postman, next to watching nonsports programming on TV, sports—on TV, radio, in print, in person, or as a participant—is our most common cultural link. [4]

The culture of sports is everywhere in America today. Sporting events touch our lives even if we don't watch or play them. Our speech is "peppered" (itself a baseball term—"to vigorously throw the ball around") with sports metaphors. Business executives and politicians regularly talk about being a "team player," "getting on base," "hitting it out of the park," "going for the score," "full-court press," "full-blitz," and "driv-

ing for the hole."[5] Sports clichés punctuate our language and
conversation, and their use supposedly reinforces the wit and
wisdom of both the originator and the person repeating the
quote. For example, Woody Hayes and/or 10,000 other college
and high school football coaches: "When the going gets tough,
the tough get going." Gary Player, golfer: "The harder you work,
the luckier you get." Ernest Hemingway, writer and angler:
"The worm lures the fish, not the fisherman and his tackle."
Yogi Berra, baseball player and coach: "If people don't want to
come out to the park, nobody's going to stop them." Vince
Lombardi, professional football coach: "Winning may not be
everything, but wanting to win is!" And, another NFL coach,
George Allen: "Losing is worse than death; you have to live with
losing."

And then, of course, there is an almost constant stream of
best-selling books by athletes, coaches, columnists, and commentators on the glory and history of the game, sports and
leadership skills, and athletics as a tool for life management. I
think we buy them because they are written by "winners" (or,
to be exact, ghostwritten by proven winner writers) and we
hope their winning ways will rub off on us. Somehow, I think,
we want to believe that if we read them, we can make our lives
better by "centering ourselves," "focusing on the ball," "bal-
ancing our inner strengths," and/or "bringing energy and
excitement to the moment."

Even how we dress reflects our passion for sports. Our
heads are covered with baseball caps from every team. We wear
football jackets in every conceivable color, material, and weight.
Basketball shirts and shorts are standard summer wear, and
high-priced gym shoes, endorsed by superstars, adorn our feet.

Allow me to offer you a series of startling figures and facts
about the effect of sports on our lives. In 1960 the four major
male professional sports of baseball, football, basketball, and
hockey had a combined attendance of 25 million fans. Since
then, the numbers have grown astronomically (See table).

	1973	1993	1997
Football	10.7 million	13.8 million	20.0 million
Baseball	30.0	70.0	65.0
Basketball	5.8	17.3	23.0
Hockey	7.6	12.7	17.0
Totals	54.1	113.8	125.0

What all this means is that, on average, in excess of 2.4 million fans attend (or at least buy tickets for) a pro sporting event each week.[6]

Although baseball, due in part to the number of games played, continues to draw the largest attendance at games, at the level of an overall audience—thanks to the omnipresent eye of the television camera—football and basketball are the most viewed sporting events in America. *Monday Night Football* on ABC is now considered a national institution. In its heyday its producers "claimed" a weekly audience of 50 million people. After thirty-three years on the air it still draws a large share of the Monday night TV audience with an 11.7 rating. (Each rating point represents 1,055,000 households that are watching the game. So if a minimum of one person per household is watching the game, that's an audience of approximately 12.5 million viewers.) In 1998, professional football's television revenues exceeded $1.2 billion, compared with about $600 million for basketball and about $300 million for baseball.[7]

Of course, the Big Kahuna of the NFL season is Super Bowl Sunday. The Super Bowl claims to be the single most-watched televised sporting event. And according to the NFL, eight of the ten most-watched television programs *ever* were Super Bowl games. Whether or not these claims are absolutely accurate, corporate marketing executives view the Super Bowl as the premier venue for reinforcing brand-name recognition and rolling out new advertisement campaigns. In Super Bowl XXXIV, January

2000, each thirty-second advertisement spot sold for 2.1 million dollars. For Super Bowl XXXV, January 2001, spots sold for 2.05 million. And for Super Bowl XXXVI, February 2002, spots sold for about 1.9 million each. Not so surprisingly, given its revenue potential, the Super Bowl game coverage is saturated with sixty commercial breaks, averaging thirty seconds in length.

Here are a few more scatter-logical facts.

- Collegiately, except for football and men's basketball, attendance at almost all other sporting events, from lacrosse to badminton, is virtually nil. (An exception is women's basketball, which traditionally has had a strong base and continues to enjoy a growing following.)
- College football attendance, from the Big 10 to Division III programs, exceeds three million people, per week.
- According to the NCAA, the college Final Four basketball tournament is the second-most-watched televised sports spectacle.
- What Americans call football is what the rest of the world calls soccer, and soccer is the most played team sport in the world.
- Officials of the World Cup (the international tournament to determine the world championship of soccer) claim that the game of soccer is both the most attended and most viewed sporting activity in the world.
- A reported 6.6 million people a year buy tickets for NASCAR's race season.
- Here's one that politicians hate: more people bowl each year than vote in congressional elections.
- And, finally, in 1995 Americans spent in excess of $55.5 billion on athletic and sports equipment, shoes, and clothing.[8]

Obviously, the driving force behind the expanded viewership and impact of sports in our lives is the media one-two punch of talk radio and television. Radio remains our most used form of public communications, and all-sports radio has been a growth industry across America for the last ten years. There are an estimated 120 radio stations in major markets across the country completely dedicated to sports talk all day long. Some of these channels also carry and cover live games, but their main focus is commentary and interaction with their audience. Besides stations totally dedicated to sports radio, there are also an estimated forty to sixty other major market stations whose programming is at least partially committed to sports talk or coverage. In Chicago for example, there are three full-time all-sports outlets and at least two others that dedicate part of their on-air programming to sports.[9]

But no matter the real impact of radio, television is the true "800-pound gorilla" when it comes to sports saturation in America. Four major networks broadcast the NFL games: CBS, FOX, ABC, and ESPN. The NBA is on ABC and several ESPN channels and other games are also shown on TNT. The NHL is on ESPN, ESPN 2, and ESPN 3 as well as on FSN and CBC (Canadian Broadcasting Company). And baseball, both locally and nationally, is just everywhere.

Before the game, of course, there are the pregame warmup shows for all the various sports on all the various channels; and let's not forget about the postgame highlights and interview shows. Then there are the national and local, all-news, all-interviews, but no call-in, sport shows. And there are the local reporters on the local half-hour news shows giving their updates. Even CNN and HBO have sports news and sport biography shows. For that matter, even demographically highbrow National Public Radio has a sports show. It's called "Only a Game," and although it is hosted by an English professor and takes a rather jaundiced view of the impact of sports on our lives as a people and a society, it's still a sports show! And if all that is not enough and you want and need more, then turn to ESPN 4 the Classics Sports Channel and watch the replay of entire games in all the major sports from the 1950s, '60s, '70s, '80s, and '90s!

With the growth of viewership, the monies generated by ticket sales, and, most important, TV revenues, individual athletes began to reap the benefits of the rising prosperity. In 1930, before the age of television, Babe Ruth was the highest paid athlete in the world. When asked if he knew that at $80,000 he was making more money than President Herbert Hoover, Ruth quipped: "I know, but I had a better year than Hoover!" Ruth's $80,000 a year established a rather exclusive benchmark for athlete salaries for decades to come. For example, in 1954, the Notre Dame running back and highly touted Heisman Trophy winner Johnny Lattner was signed by the Pittsburgh Steelers for $12,500, which included his signing bonus and his salary.[10]

As late as the 1960s, ordinary players in professional sports were not paid much more than ordinary blue-collar workers. Even the giants of their particular sports earned, by today's standard, relatively small dollars. (For example, in 1964 Wilt Chamberlain was reportedly making 1 million dollars a year.) Moreover, not all of the superstars were automatically making super money. According to the baseball historian David Seiderman, Mickey Mantle (arguably one of the best athletes ever to play the game) never topped Joe DiMaggio's $100,000 salary throughout his long, eighteen-year career.[11]

By the mid-1970s all athletes' pay began to climb rapidly. And the superstars in their respective sports not only earned large salaries but also commanded huge fees for product endorsements, commercials, and other media work. Some of these "media-jocks" began generating incomes rivaling the achievements of wunderkind Bill Gates. For example, in his last year as a member of the Chicago Bulls, Michael Jordan's base salary was $35 million. In addition, in his last five years of playing for the Bulls, he reportedly earned in excess of $150 million a year—above and beyond his salary—in endorsements and business investments.[12] To put it all in perspective, in 1970 the average baseball player earned $125,000, the average football player $99,000, and the average basketball player $43,000.

In 1997 the baseball players averaged $1.4 million, football players $754,000, and basketball players $2.3 million.[13] And that's before they stepped on a soundstage and some producer for "product X" yelled: "Lights! Camera! Action!"

As a race, our fascination with sports has a long history which predates the mass exposure of radio and television and the continuous barrage of hype from marketers and merchandisers. The modern Olympic Games had their birth in ancient Greece. Long before the Los Angeles Coliseum and Chicago's Soldier Field, different kinds of athlete/warriors fought for victory in Rome's Coliseum. And before Michael Jordan perfected his slam dunk, the Incas of Machu Picchu had developed a crude precursor to the game of basketball.

Nevertheless, a series of related questions beg to be answered. Why are we so fascinated with sports and athletes? Why is it so easy to get lost in sports? Why have sports become such a large part of our lives? I think that there are *at least* four possible answers to these questions.

1. To be fair, there is an upside to our collective passion for sports, which all too often gets overlooked or forgotten. Putting aside the particular game or event involved, there is a natural beauty and rhythm to sports which is really all about the celebration of the abilities of the human body. The various "languages of the body" as demonstrated in a hundred-yard dash, a full-court press, a deep pass downfield, or in the ballet-like moves of gymnastics can be a thing of grace, poetry, and beauty. The agility, flexibility, strength, and preparation required for the performance of any athletic event, can offer both the casual and the committed fan a moment of true aesthetic awe, admiration, and delight.

2. Although sports can offer a career to only a relative handful of athletes, playing sports can teach any and every athlete important lessons about life. To begin with, and lest we forget, sports is about play! Psychologically, to play is to extend oneself. To use one's imagination. To get out of oneself. Psychologists tell us that children need play in order to safely examine the world. They need play to learn, grow, and fulfill themselves as persons. Besides being fun, play is supposed to be challenging, expansive, expressive, and growthful. Plato, in his classic works *The Republic* and *The Laws*, argues that the purpose of sports is to teach *completion, coordination,* and *cooperation.*

Completion:	• The use and testing of one's body.
	• To extend, expand one's range of physical abilities.
	• To learn the limits of one's endurance and abilities.
	• To learn to be comfortable in one's body.
Coordination:	• To synchronize body and mind.
	• To anticipate.
	• To image, to visualize.
	• To plan, to strategize.
Cooperation:	(Sports teaches:)
	• Community effort.
	• Collective behavior.
	• Teamwork.

The concepts of completion, coordination, cooperation, and competition are intimately connected. The Latin word for competition is *competere*, "to seek together." The modern cliché "There is no I in TEAM" is wrong; or, at least, it's only literally true. There is an "I" in "TEAM," in fact, many "I's." The trick is to learn how to blend the energy, initiative, and ability of the various "I's" involved in the pursuit of the same goal.

For Plato, all children, girls and boys alike, must participate in sports. Sports, he argued, is a necessary ingredient in the formation of both the individual person and the collective community. The concepts of self, citizen, and sports participation were, for Plato, indivisibly conjoined. This is exactly why General Douglas MacArthur, when he was commandant of West Point, required all cadets to participate in a team sport. As a student of history, MacArthur was convinced it was on the playing fields of Eton (England) that the British officer class learned the lessons of *completion, coordination,* and *cooperation* which ultimately enabled them to defeat Napoleon at Waterloo.

3. Sports are something we do or view "for the love of it," "for its own sake alone," "for the joy of the doing." At their best, sports offer a benign distraction, simple entertainment, an escape, or a buffer against the realities of the everyday world. In the words of the Jewish philosopher Baruch Spinoza: "Give men an open field, a ball to catch or kick or something or someone to chase, and they are happy, despite all else."

Sports are a hobby we can *supposedly* safely and easily devote ourselves to. *Theoretically,* one doesn't have to take a lot of time off, travel a great deal, or spend tons of money to engage in or be a spectator at a sporting event. The words *supposedly* and *theoretically,* of course, are open to wide interpretation. For example, in the summer of 2001 the average cost for a Chicago family of four to spend the day at a Cubs game in Wrigley Field from tickets to transportation was approximately $175. Just two tickets to a Bears football game or a Blackhawk hockey game can cost you $100 before you pay for parking, pizza, popcorn, and/or beer. Those of you who are golfers, skiers, or scuba divers know full well that time, travel, and equipment are not minor considerations. These are the high-end sporting activities that require planning, preparation, and plenty of cash. At the other end of the spectrum, you don't need much more than a decent pair of gym shoes and some comfortable clothing to go jogging or get involved in a pickup game of baseball or basketball. I suspect that most of us seek an athletic outlet somewhere between these two extremes by joining a fitness or racquet club or by taking exercise classes at the local Y.

Costs aside, I think we are drawn to sports, find amusement and pleasure in them because sports fulfill the historian Johan Huizinga's three criteria for "true play." (1) Sports stand outside our mundane day-to-day lives. (2) Sports represent a kind of freedom of expression, a chance for openness and creativity. (3) Finally, the rules are clear and self-contained, and winning or losing is clear and obvious.[14] As a form of play, sports are a way of doing something and nothing at the same time. For the spectator, sports is a form of "eye candy," voyeurism, titillation. It is a way of losing yourself without getting totally lost in the process. There is, of course, a danger connected to all of this. In devoting ourselves to a private passion which is out of proportion to its real importance, we can deaden ourselves to issues that truly matter and deserve our attention.[15]

4. The longtime loquacious sports analyst Howard Cosell once said that Americans love sports because sports are a self-chosen microcosm of reality. He went on to say that on the "field of play" most, if not all, of the central issues and values of life are acted out and resolved. Each game, each contest, he said, is a "mini-muscle and mind morality play" with "good guys" (our team), "bad guys" (their team), and a "jury" (fans) who can boo or cheer as they see fit. And, suggested Cosell, all of this occurs in a totally structured, self-contained environment with a clear winner and loser. (Vince Lombardi was right, "A tie is like kissing your sister!" It's a kiss, but it doesn't do anything for you!) Cosell believed (I think regretfully) that many fans do not look at sports as just a hobby, a diversion, or as a metaphor for life, but as a substitute for life, reality itself, and, for some, a religion.

The scholar and sportswriter Gerald Early agrees. He suggests that the rhythms, rites, and rituals of sports are seductive to postmodern society because they transcend the confusion, complexity, and uncertainty of everyday life. The world of sports for the true believer, says Early, does not just offer momentary diversion or a brief reprieve from the chaos of the world but rather "eternal salvation through the creation and total substitution of an alternative reality, the universe of sports."[16]

I think Cosell and Early are right; many of us are drawn to sports because it is a self-contained manageable universe with its own language and logic. It is a universe of clearly defined rules and regulations, of specified goals and objectives. It is a universe of ever-changing tactics and strategy that can be endlessly analyzed and studied. It is a universe that can be quantified and measured, and whose statistics are often as seductively interesting as the actual game being played. At least for the spectators, if not the participants, it is also a universe that is sanitized and safe (except for English soccer fans and perhaps the "bleacher bums" at Wrigley Field). It is a universe of controlled and understandable chaos. It is a universe where everything and nothing are simultaneously at stake—just ask Bill Buckner of the Boston Red Sox (the error that cost them the World Series) or Jim Kelly of the Buffalo Bills (four trips to the Super Bowl, zero wins). It is a universe where the "divinities of the game" are media accessible and intimately knowable to the fans and true believers. (On January 4, 2002, half of the newspapers in America featured front-page, not just sports-page, coverage of The Petition for Dissolution of Marriage: Juanita Jordan v. Michael Jordan.) It is a universe that is able to impose absolute order and clarity by the efficient and final means of a win/loss column. It is a universe where the bottom line is always clear and irrevocable: Winners talk! Losers walk!

Our collective passion for sports, and our use of sports as a means to achieving leisure and escape, is not hard to understand. The universe of sports allows us to find a niche, establish a place, and create order in an often chaotic and unwelcoming world. Being a Yankee fan or Bear booster allows us to establish a way of being in the world. It gives us an identity, a purpose, and a (team) logo.

What is more, the leitmotiv, mottos, and mantras of sports simultaneously reinforce and reflect the general values of our socioeconomic system. Under capitalism the rugged individual is the ideal. Cutthroat competition and social Darwinism are the natural order of things. And we believe that in the long run the winner-takes-all mentality results in the greatest possible good for the greatest possible number. To paraphrase the words of George Will, sports in general, and especially football, combines elements of everything that appeals to Americans. There is competition, action, speed, and violence, which is punctuated by committee meetings, followed by the establishment of a winner and loser, and endless insider analysis and commentary.

One definition of a "fanatic" is a person who needs to believe in something larger than himself or herself, and does so with extreme and often uncritical enthusiasm. But one does not have to be a fanatic to want to be taken out of oneself, to want to be committed, or to get lost in something greater than oneself. The desire to be part of something more—whatever that more is— may be as human and as elemental as the desire to know and the need for food, water, and shelter.

It is easy to get lost in sports. It is easy to form an emotional attachment to teams and players. It is easy to get caught up in the spectacle of the games. Sports may not be a morality play or a metaphor for real life, but they are far easier to deal with and eminently more understandable than real life. Sports remain one of the few areas in life where clear victories and exact outcomes are yet possible. Is it any wonder that we find them so appealing, and all too often so irresistible?

In *Being and Time*, Martin Heidegger suggested that in lieu of being able to address and understand the serious questions and issues of life, we busy ourselves with cocktail party conversations and escapist behavior. For good or ill, the statistics are incontrovertible: Americans love their games and adore and idealize their athlete/warriors and gladiator/heroes.

seven

The Ultimate Vacation
RETIREMENT

I've got enough money now to retire, but I'm not about to. Work
keeps me going. It's the only thing I really like or know. How
many times a week can I go golfing? How many vacations a year
can I take? What am I supposed to do with myself? Forget it! I'm
staying on the job. I don't want to get old and die too soon!

—*J. Dwayne Roush*

Trying to define what we mean by retirement is like trying to
pinpoint the exact meaning of happiness; everyone you talk to
and every resource you consult will offer a slightly different
definition or description. The only absolute we can be assured
of, according to the psychologist U. V. Manion, is that the phenomenon of retirement, like vacations, is a direct by-product of
a postmodern industrial society.[1]

Until the early part of the twentieth century most people
worked until they were no longer able, because they had no
other alternative. It wasn't really until the Roosevelt administration pushed through the Social Security Act in 1935, the general
proliferation of union contracts and benefits, and the emergence
of private pension plans and investment funds that retirement
for the common worker became a realistic possibility.

As with the concepts of work and vacations, we are as a people and a society deeply conflicted or maybe just unsure and scared about retirement and what it will mean for us. But time without work—whether dreaded or longed for—is something that all of us, if we're lucky, will have to deal with sooner or later.[2] Some people, of course, look forward to retirement. They see it as the ultimate vacation. Retirement to them means the end of mandatory labor and the beginning of a truly free life. My father is one of these people. My dad is not a man of many words. He never talked much with anyone, including my mother or myself. I've probably only had five serious conversations with my father, and all of them were about work. (Being laconic, he, of course, skipped right over the traditional "father and teenage son let's talk about sex" conversation. Luckily, I had an older cousin who had access to *National Geographic* magazines, so I did get an overview of the basics). My dad talked to me, actually he lectured to me, about: working hard, doing your duty, taking care of your wife and family (I guess he figured my cousin or somebody would fill me in about all of that), doing the job right, not being a trouble maker, keeping up with your union dues, and, to my utter surprise, retiring as soon as possible! The first time he said it to me, I was shocked. "Retire," I said to him, "you're joking? You're a working machine. You're never home. You've got two jobs. Retirement! What are you talking about?"

"Yeah! Yeah!" he said to me. "So I put a lot of time in on the job. It's not because I want to. You got to work to live. Don't we live in a nice place?" he asked. "Don't we have food on the table? Aren't you in college?" "Yes, but—" I protested. "But nothing," he said. "It's just that simple. And don't forget I grew up in the Depression and then I went right into the service. When I got out, jobs were a perk and not a guarantee. So, when I eventually got the job at the Post Office—I worked hard to protect it so I could take care of your mother and you."

"The truth is," he confided to me in whispered tones, "I hated the Post Office. But," he went on to explain, "they never ever fired civil service workers, so it was guaranteed, steady work. And best of all," he beamed, "I knew the exact day that I could retire on full pension, so I'd never have to go back to that place again. Hey, kid" (he *never, ever* addressed me by my first name) "that's what work's about. Put your time in, put a little money in the bank, and when the day comes you'll be able to collect your pension and your social security check each month like clockwork."

For my father's generation, Tom Brokaw's "The Greatest Generation," work was both a boon and a burden; something you needed to do but not something you necessarily liked doing. In the words of Studs Terkel, for my dad, work was a "Monday through Friday sort of dying."[3] My dad's goals were clear and simple: survival, a modicum of success, and the sweet idyll of a swing, a back porch, and never having to work again. For my dad, retirement was the reward of freedom, after years of labor, and being a prisoner of work.

In many ways my dad's attitude about work and retirement reminds me of the story that NPR correspondent Daniel Schorr once told about Senator Kennedy of Massachusetts. "When Ted Kennedy ran for the Senate the first time, his opponent accused him of having never worked a day in his life. The next day while shaking hands at a factory, one of the older workers looked Kennedy in the eyes and said: 'Don't worry about it kid, you haven't missed a thing!'" Some say this story is just an urban legend. No matter, even if it's a myth, its message, I think, remains clear: Most of us work because we have to, not because we want to. If you're smart or, just lucky, you'll quit as soon as you can.

There are some folks, of course, who so love their work that they could not imagine life or happiness without it. For these individuals, the very concept of permanent retirement or per- manent vacation constitutes their definition of permanent bore-

dom. These are the folks who'd be in complete agreement with George Bernard Shaw's admonition: "A perpetual holiday is a good working definition of hell." Retirement for them is the gateway to the great existential vacuum of uselessness, despair, and ennui. After all, if you are what you do, who are you, what are you if you don't do anything at all?[4]

Robert Reich tells the story of man named Milton Garland, who at the age of 102 was the oldest-known wage earner in America. Garland had worked for the same firm, the Frick Company of Waynesboro, Pennsylvania (a manufacturer and installer of refrigeration equipment) for seventy-eight years. "I love the work I'm doing," said Garland, referring to his current twenty-hour-a-week job supervising patent development and training young workers. "My advice," he said, "is to go into something and stay with it until you obtain expertise in the work. And once you are an expert, it's a pleasure." Asked where he would be if he had retired thirty-seven years earlier at the age of sixty-five, Garland snapped back without a moment's hesitation, "In my grave!"[5]

Then there are the people who don't necessarily love their work, or even like it, but they are so linked to it that life without it, retirement, is both unthinkable and unbearable. These are people whose entire identity is wrapped up in what they do. These are people for whom work is their only calling card to the rest of the world. These are people who see losing work (for any reason) as a fall from grace, a loss of status and identity. These are people for whom retirement means becoming a DP (displaced person) or more accurately a FIP (formerly important person). Some, but not all, FIPs fear and loathe retirement because it forces them to ask a series of very difficult questions of themselves: "Who am I now?" "How do I introduce myself?" "What's my purpose or reason for being?"

The novelist Hans Habe has argued that a person's work is not like a suit of clothes an individual can take off and yet remain the same person they were before. Jobs, he said, are like our skin that we cannot take off without bleeding to death.[6] As the sociologist Robert Kahn has so poignantly put it:

> When people ask that most self-identifying of questions—Who am I?—they answer in terms of their occupation: toolmaker, press operator, typist, doctor, construction worker, teacher. Even people who are not working identify themselves by their former work or their present wish for it, describing themselves as retired or unemployed. [7]

Then there are those who dread retirement as the beginning of the end. They rank it right up there with the other big life markers of death, divorce, downsizing (joblessness), and debilitation. They see it as a sentence, a penalty, and not a perk. They see it as being put out to pasture to await death in as comfortable a circumstance as possible.

The gerontologist David Gutmann has suggested that for some people, regardless of their bank accounts or surroundings, retirement is the first institutional "insult" of aging and represents tangible evidence that one is publicly recognized as elderly.[8] According to the social psychologist Walli Leff, the "mythic pre-eminence of the work ethic as a basic American value" confers both a social and a moral obligation on us to work, and conversely causes us to often scorn, patronize, or pity those who don't work for whatever reason. The retired person, says Leff, is often categorized as a second-class citizen, a former player, a former worker, regardless of the individual's abilities, prior achievements, or financial status.[9] Too many retirees are looked at as quaint curiosities. They may be admired, but they are at best discarded survivors.

In a culture dominated by youth, novelty, change, and disposability, many people, rightly or wrongly, see retirement as a curtailment of their rights and options both as a worker and as a person. They may also see it as taking away a part of their life they may not yet want to give up. As one bitter retiree told me:

> Oh sure, they throw you one hell of a retirement party—big speeches, testimonials, gag gifts, and serious gifts too. They tell you how important you are, how they don't know how they'll function without you, and how you'll be called back in so much as a consultant that it will seem like you never really retired. Right! Right! And—then—then, nothing! No calls, no questions, no consulting, no "Hello, how are you?," nothing! It's as if they don't know you anymore. It's as if—you're dead already.

And finally, there's another group of people who don't want to retire, but not because of financial or psychological desperation or need, or because they feel disenfranchised without a job title. Rather, they do not want to quit because they don't want to give up their creative outlet and a chance to contribute to others. These are folks who don't necessarily fear death, but they do agree with Eleanor Roosevelt when she said: "When you cease to make a contribution, you begin to die."

Now, let me be very clear about this. I'm not talking about pure altruists, saints, or cadres of Mother Teresa clones who are singularly committed to the well-being of others and without any concern for themselves. I'm not talking exclusively about high-minded or heroic surgeons, social workers, firefighters, police officers, teachers, clergy or any type of profession or jobs that are service-based and directly affect the well-being of others. I'm talking about any job, any profession, task, or trade in which the worker thinks the work worth doing and thinks that justice requires that it should be done well. Usually, but not always, these are people who love what they do or, at the very least, believe what they do is worthwhile or necessary.

These are the people, suggested John Dewey, for whom work has become permeated with an attitude of play and is no longer drudgery but art—even if they themselves would never consciously call it art.[10] These are people who stay at it because they can, because they want to, and because for them "the doing is as important as what gets done, the making as valuable as what gets made."[11] These are the people who embody and live out, both the letter and the spirit of John Gardner's admonition:

> The society that scorns excellence in plumbing because it is a
> humble activity, yet accepts shoddiness in philosophy because it
> is an exalted activity, will have neither good plumbing nor good
> philosophy, and as a result, neither its pipes nor its theories will
> hold water.[12]

According to the U.S. Census Bureau, 2.9 percent of the full-time civilian workforce, or 3,882,000 persons, is made up of individuals sixty-five years of age or older. As I have indicated, some of these individuals must work out of need and necessity, but a growing number of individuals stay on the job or take on new jobs because they want to. For example, Carl Dubbs, sixty-nine, is interim police chief of Roselle, Illinois. It's the third job he's held since he officially retired. "I worked in Wheaton for 28 years and retired in March 1996," he said. "Then I went to Northlake from September 1997 until June 1998. Before coming here to Roselle, I took a job in Bensenville from May through September of 1999. I enjoy what I'm doing and have devoted my life to it," says Dobbs. "It's the most rewarding thing I've ever done. Believe me, I'm here because I want to be here; it's not about the money. I still got a contribution to make and there's nothing more rewarding than having the opportunity to make a difference in society."[13]

Besides those retirees who refuse to retire, there is another growing category of retirees who are willing to quit work only on a part-time basis. These are typically folks who want to stop working at what they've always done, but don't want to be entirely inactive. Many of these individuals take on jobs that require only a few hours a day or a few days a week. They take jobs that they find interesting, offer a challenge, or simply give them something to do. According to the nationwide Ignation (Jesuit) Volunteer Corps, growing numbers of individuals are volunteering to work for their communities, for their churches, and in their local school systems. As one volunteer- worker-retiree put it: "I've had a very successful life. I've been lucky, and not everyone is. So I figure this is a way to give something back. Don't get me wrong I'm no goodie-two-shoes and I'm certainly not a religious fanatic, but doing nothing for the rest of my life seems like a sin to me."[14]

According to my friend and GQ columnist Terry Sullivan, the happiest people he knows are people who don't retire because they get paid to do what they want to do. Therefore, he advises everyone to find a job doing something you wouldn't want to stop doing and die happily in harness. After all, he says, Picasso didn't retire to play golf, so why should you? Think about it, some of the best jobs in the world don't even have a retirement plan—pope, queen, Supreme Court justice, a Rolling Stone![15]

As we make our way in the twenty-first century it's important to realize as a nation that how we look at age, aging, work, leisure and retirement has been radically affected by relatively recent breakthroughs in science, medicine, and our general standard of living. And all of these factors have had a profound impact on how we live, how many of us are alive, and how long we can expect to go on living.

The 2000 Census statistics depict a demographic reality I doubt even futurists such as Jules Verne or George Orwell could have foreseen. Not only are more of us living than ever before (281,421,906), more of us are living longer than ever before. In 1900, the average life expectancy in America was 47 years old, and in 2000, the average was 76. And we are not only living longer, we are growing older as a nation. Fully 50.4 percent of our population, or 142,092,916 people, are 35 years old or older. The average age of an American is now 35.3 years old, which is 2.4 years older than we were a decade ago, and 12 years older than we were a century ago.[16]

But clearly the most startling demographic statistic altering our social and economic landscape is the number of those individuals born in the afterglow of World War II. These are individuals between the ages of 35 and 57, who now number 82,826,479 strong and represent 29.4 percent of the U.S. population—the omnipresent baby boomers! Since 1946 boomers have been the undigested rabbit in the python. They have been the unspoken impetus behind the growth of suburbia, shopping malls, highways, hospitals, schools, libraries, universities, and a whole host of complex infrastructures beyond enumeration. Boomers are the most measured, monitored, massaged, managed, manipulated, and most fully documented generation ever. They are the dominant demographic that has generated a long list of "firsts."

- Best educated
- Most prosperous

- Healthiest
- Most mortgaged (homes, cars, credit cards)
- Most addicted (drugs, alcohol, consumer goods)
- Most divorced
- Fewest number of children
- Most rebellious
- Most cynical
- Most media bombarded

Many of these boomers fought in or against our most unpopular war, Vietnam. Many dropped out and joined the Age of Aquarius. More of them got hip, high, and wise and went to college. Lots and lots of them became solid middle-class citizens and the moms and dads of Generations X and Y. And as of January 1, 1996, every 8.4 seconds another boomer turns 50 years old, thereby putting mounting pressure on an under-staffed and underfunded Social Security and Medicare system. (Aristotle was wrong. Numbers can put people into a "passion," especially if you're a number cruncher working for Congress or a regulatory agency trying to figure out how you're going to fund the onslaught of retirement and medical benefits coming due starting in 2011.)

Not only have the raw numbers changed, but how we per-ceive age and how we react to it have been dramatically altered because we are not only living longer, but also living healthier, more active lives than ever before. In the 1930s, H. L. Mencken lamented that after you're 40 years old, it's all over. "The best years are the 40s," he said. "After that, a person begins to dete-riorate. But in their 40s, people are at the zenith of their energy and vitality." For Mencken, 40 meant middle age, and middle age meant crisis, breakdown and the beginnings of old age and death.

In the late 1960s, Margaret Mead told a Senate subcommit-tee on aging that "in this society, women retire, men die." Men die, she suggested, some five to seven years before their wives, for two simple reasons. To begin with, they are burned out, worn out, or made old long before their time because of the hours and difficulties of their working life. Second, and ironically, they die of boredom and despair because no matter how bad their work, their work is the only thing they really know and their only means of achieving self-respect and identity. Without work, they have nothing to do and were nothing. (When Mead made her comments, the approximate average life expectancy for males was 67 years and 74 years for females. At the time, less than 30 percent of all women worked full-time.)

As recently as 1978, the psychologist Daniel J. Levinson in his landmark book *Seasons of a Man's Life* created a chronology, a timeline, a yardstick by which we measure and delineate the different phases in human development. (Although Levinson's thesis primarily dealt with males, many of his theories, life patterns, and developmental models were also applicable to women.) Levinson postulated that human life was divided into four distinct life stages: Pre-Adulthood (0–17), Early Adulthood (17–40), Middle Adulthood (40–60), and Late Adulthood (60–?), as shown in the figure below.

Each of these stages, argued Levinson, contains its own specific set of tasks and challenges. Each stage and each step within each stage constitute the building blocks of individual personality and identity. We measure ourselves and are measured by others, said Levinson, by how well we accomplish the tasks of each of the stages of our life, as well as the fluidity of the transitions that we make between the various stages of development.

While considered cutting-edge at the time of its publication, Levinson's chronology of human development and decline seems in retrospect to be not only a tad gender-biased but also negatively archaic and pessimistic in regard to the numbers. Specifically, Levinson's Late Adulthood is made up of two stages. Stage I, Late Adulthood: Transition (60–65) was about *settling in* and *settling up* accounts. It was about finding satisfaction or

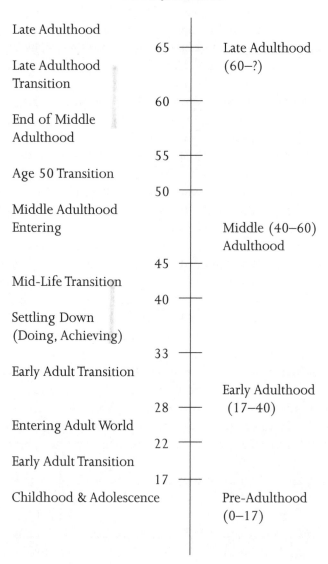

Seasons of a Man's Life
Daniel J. Levinson

Late Adulthood

65 — Late Adulthood
(60–?)
Late Adulthood
Transition

60 —

End of Middle
Adulthood

55 —

Age 50 Transition

50 —

Middle Adulthood
Entering   Middle (40–60)
Adulthood

45 —

Mid-Life Transition

40 —

Settling Down
(Doing, Achieving)

33 —

Early Adult Transition

Early Adulthood
28 —   (17–40)

Entering Adult World

22 —

Early Adult Transition

17 —

Childhood & Adolescence   Pre-Adulthood
(0–17)

disappointment in our lifestyles and life choices. It was about carrying on and doing one's duty or falling apart. Stage II, Late Adulthood (65–?), was, said Levinson, final accounting time. It was about living with our fruits or our failures. It was about memories, reflections, preparing for death. For Levinson, anything and everything that happened after 65 was seen as a bonus or a perk.[17]

Personally, I don't think Levinson's numbers or chronology were either myopic or intentionally maudlin. They were simply a reflection of his data and his experience. People did die earlier then; people did age sooner. Nevertheless, whether intentional or not, his research did help to perpetuate the myth that elderly people were frail, useless, unproductive, and finished. In so doing, he reinforced our traditional and unrealistic fear about aging.

Happily, within twenty years of the publication of *Seasons of a Man's Life*, demographic surveys and research began to report on a new timeline for human development and offer a new perspective on aging. In 1998, Gail Sheehy published *Understanding Men's Passages*, and in 1999, the MacArthur Foundation Research Network released a report on *Successful Midlife Development*. Both of these publications paint a new portrait of aging and offer new models, metaphors, and maps to help plan out and navigate our newly extended lives.

Sheehy posits a new timeline that not only updates Levinson's numbers but also redefines our lifestyle choices and options as we age. She argues that thanks to advances in general medicine, nutrition, biotechnology, and brain research, we will be routinely able to extent our lives well into our eighties and ninties. And, she argues, this newly acquired longevity will not be years of loss, loneliness, debilitation, and illness. They can and will be years, she says, full of vision, vitality, and, yes, sometimes Viagra too![18]

Look around, says Sheehy, everyone is staying younger longer, and it's not just a matter of designer drugs, cosmetic surgery, and the fashion industry. Thirty-year-olds have the energy of recent college grads; forty-year-olds can compete with thirty-year-olds; fifty is what forty used to be; and sixty is what fifty was. Men and women who are fifty today, says Sheehy, and remain free of cancer and heart disease can expect to live to between eighty-seven and ninety-two with some vigor. With each decade of research, says Sheehy, we are adding months and years to the longevity tables. In comparison to our parents' and grandparents' generations, we have acquired an added life—what Sheehy calls our "second adulthood."

Sheehy's complete timeline looks something like the next figure.

Ten years of research in psychology, sociology, anthropology, and medicine went into the MacArthur Foundation project on *Successful Midlife Development*. The project's report essentially confirms and reinforces Sheehy's figures and findings. The baby boomers are the test case proving the point, says the report. Aided by advances in science and the good fortune of "good times," boomers are living longer and better lives than any generation before them. By the year 2050, the average life expectancy of men and women will reach eighty-nine years, up from seventy-five years in 1995.

Moreover, as boomers age and birth rates decline, they are seriously altering the age range of the nation. In 2020, people over the age of sixty-five will increase from 35 million in 1995 to 53 million. In 2026, people over the age of eighty-five will increase to 9 million from 4.2 million in 1999. And by 2020, senior boomers will make up more than 18 percent of the U.S. population—the same proportion as in Florida today.[19] Of course, as the report points out, individual longevity is dependent on a number of variables: health, habits, wealth, attitude, energy, environment, and relationships. Clearly, however, for us as individuals and a society, the duration, structure, and options available in our lives are changing.

So we are all (we hope) living longer and better. There are,

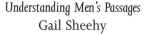

Understanding Men's Passages
Gail Sheehy

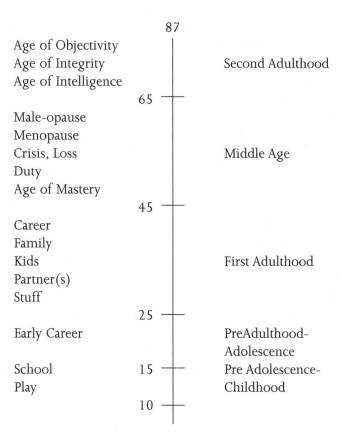

	87	
Age of Objectivity		
Age of Integrity		Second Adulthood
Age of Intelligence		
	65	
Male-opause		
Menopause		
Crisis, Loss		Middle Age
Duty		
Age of Mastery		
	45	
Career		
Family		
Kids		First Adulthood
Partner(s)		
Stuff		
	25	
Early Career		PreAdulthood-Adolescence
School	15	Pre Adolescence-Childhood
Play		
	10	

of course, a few critical questions that need to be answered. What are we going to do with this new gift of life? How are we going to handle our second adulthood? Shall we just carry on as usual? Just keep doing more of the same? Will our work continue to be our primary preoccupation? Will we continue to outwork the Europeans, the Japanese, the world? Will we continue to accept the feverish pace of work and make our jobs the primary recipient of our interests, our ingenuity, and our energies?

Robert Reich adds to the chorus of questions when he asks: Shall we allow the almost ubiquitous intrusion of phones, faxes, beepers, and e-mails on our professional and personal lives to continue apace? Can we turn them off, let up on the accelerator, slow down the adrenaline flow? Are we so defined by our jobs that we have no identity or sense of self-esteem when we are without a job? Are we valued only because we produce? Do we have status only because we contribute to the economy? If we are roleless, jobless, will our family, friends, community think of us, as at best, an ornament of some sentimental value; or, at worst, as a throwaway, used-up, no longer productive object?[20] Shall we just accept the notion forced upon us in the past that as responsible adults, we are to plan our lives around work, and not work around our lives? Shall we just keep our present preoccupations, keep being on, keep doing, keep—whatever until we burn out or die?[21] Personally, I hope and pray that we won't; or, at the very least, that I won't, but according to demographers at the Hudson Institute, some of us may have to!

Both the French philosopher and mathematician Auguste Comte and the American economist and coauthor of *Workforce 2020* Richard W. Judy agree that "demographics is destiny." Surely, there is more to destiny than just numbers, but when it comes to the supply of labor, numbers and demography are certainly determinant. The bottom line here, says Judy, is obvious and critical. Not only are there more of us than ever before, and more of us living longer than ever before, now, for the first time in American history, there are more older and middle-aged people than there are younger people. And, says Judy, this trend will continue well into the twenty-first century.[22]

According to Judy, between now and the year 2020, the movement of boomers into their fifties and sixties will most significantly affect the age compositions of both the population and the workforce. The 55 to 64 age group will nearly double between now and then. And, beginning in 2011, when the first boomers reach 65 years old, the ranks of America's elderly will explode. All of these changes, says Judy, will profoundly alter the appearance and performance of the American population in many ways.

Judy argues that perhaps the most important consequence of our aging population is that the number of working-age individuals available to support each person of retirement age will plunge dramatically in the early years of the twenty-first century. There are now more than 4.5 persons aged 20 to 64 for each person 65 years or older. After 2010, however, as boomers age into their late sixties and beyond, that critical ratio will fall sharply before leveling off at slightly above 2.5 around 2030.

To the extent that all these "geezer boomers" (Judy's term, not mine!) actually manage to retire, says Judy, the falling "worker-to-elder" ratio implies a rapidly growing burden on the remaining population. The fiscal strain of mushrooming senior entitlements—Social Security, Medicare, etc.—will be unsustainable. Ergo, Judy concludes, "geezerhood" ain't going to be what it used to be. People are going to *need* to work longer. Of course, he points out, many "geezers" will *want* to work longer because they will be in good health and won't like being idle. But at the very least, says Judy, most "geezer entitlements" are going to need to be whittled back a great deal. And, he says, we will also need new alternative mental models for the so-called retirement years.[23]

Webster's New Collegiate Dictionary defines retirement as "withdrawal from work or business because of age . . . ." "To retire . . . to fall back, to recede." This definition is part of the archaic thinking that surrounds age, aging, and retirement. Given the new demographics, a new definition needs to be created and a new series of questions needs to be asked. Doesn't a longer life offer more opportunities for second and third careers and chances? Shouldn't we begin talking about retirement versus second retirement, and partial retirements and retiring in phases, or what are called retirement rehearsals? Consider the following editorial by Dave Patel that recently appeared in *HR Magazine* (see inset).[24]

Ken Dychtwald argues in his upbeat and provocative book *AgeWave* that the concept of "first and final" retirement is part of our long-held cultural "misbeliefs, prejudices, and phobias we share regarding aging." Collectively, says Dychtwald, too many of us have a mental "blueprint" of age and aging which is negative, dated, or simply not accurate. As boomers turn into "geezers," says Dychtwald, we collectively need to address these myths about aging and correct them so that we free ourselves from our self-imposed gerontophobia.

> Myth I: People over 65 are old.
> Myth II: Most older people are chronically in poor
>   health.
> Myth III: Older minds are not as bright and flexible
>   as younger minds.
> Myth IV: Older people are undependable and
>   unproductive.
> Myth V: Older people are unattractive and sexless.
> Myth VI: All older people are pretty much the same.
> Myth VII: All older people lose their passion for life.[25]

Deloss Marsh, in *Retirement Careers*, also talks about the myths and misconceptions surrounding aging and retirement and offers a series of tips and suggestions for combining the best of work and leisure in our "retirement years." To begin with, says Marsh, too many of us enter retirement as if we were the first ones ever to do so. Naively, we expect the simply fact of unspecified/unencumbered leisure to fill our days with satisfaction and contentment. Then, we soon discover, as many have before, that satisfaction doesn't come from leisure alone. Marsh suggests that people used to prepare for retirement primarily by fully funding and carefully nurturing their pension plans, private savings, and Social Security accounts. Now we need to do

Rearranging the Life Cycle
By Dave Patel

Today's average employee works for 45 years, beginning work life at about age 20 and working until the age of 65, and enjoys retirement for another 15 years. This system is tied into the fabric of American lives, affecting everything from education, compensation, taxation, health care, housing, transportation and retirement planning.

Now consider an alternative method of work, still taking into account working for 45 years but breaking that 45-year block into two or three segments. Wouldn't you rather take 10 years off at age 35, going back to work at age 45, then taking another five years off at age 60, and then working from 65–80?

Impossible, you say.

Where would their income come from? What about health care? Taxes? Who wants to work until they're 80? All legitimate questions, but the changing realities of the aging workforce may necessitate a paradigm shift such as the one envisioned above.

Consider that today's notions of work date from the Industrial Age, our school year is based on an agrarian economy, and the health care system still focuses on prohibitively expensive medical technology, instead of investing in preventative systems that enable healthier daily living. As for working until the age of 80, consider that when President Franklin Roosevelt set the retirement age at 65, average life expectancy in the United States was 63. Life expectancy today is at 76 and climbing.

Numbers influence policies, and much of our socioeconomic life for the past 50 years has been greatly influenced by the sheer numbers of the baby boom generation.

continued

As the 80 million boomers age, what they want to do in their "retirement" years may end up redefining concepts of work and retirement. Contingent work, part-time work, portable health care, transportation assistance, focus on wellness instead of emergency medical procedures, private Social Security accounts and lifelong learning all could become commonplace.

For more information, on emerging issues, visit www.shrm.org/trends.

David Patel is the manager of workplace trends and forecasting at the Society for Human Resource Managers.

a lot more than that, says Marsh. We need to plan and prepare for retirement in ways we never had to before.

The reality is people need a reason for getting up each morning. There needs to be some purpose or focus to the day. Too many of us assume, says Marsh, that we can indulge in our leisure passions full-time. We naively believe that a daily diet of travel, fishing, golf, sailing, or the pursuit of a long-cherished hobby will make us happy and keep us satisfied. However, most of us, but not all of us, quickly find out that these passions, these creative outlets, even when we can afford them, are not enough, in themselves, to sustain us.

Marsh argues that we need to work and plan for our retirements with the same intensity that we plotted out our careers. In fact, he says, we have to make our retirement our career. What we have to do, says Marsh, is carefully assess what we have and what we need in order to figure out what we want to do with our lives.[26]

Gail Sheehy believes that living out our second adulthood, our "retirement careers," is a boon and not a burden because our second adulthood can be free of the mistakes and miscues of our first adulthood. Our second adulthood, says Sheehy, offers us the opportunity, in Plato's words, to put aside "the passions and indiscretions of youth" so that we can:

- Learn the lesson and walk away from the pain.
- See beyond unimportant parochial particulars.
- Let go of some of our self-serving egoism.
- Transcend pointless power struggles.
- No longer fear failure.
- No longer always have to worry about self-aggrandizement.
- No longer be solely involved in careers, status, success.
- Be open to the possibility/reality of change.
- Be non-threatened by the needs of others.
- Be open to different life lessons.

Abraham Maslow once suggested that wisdom was the accumulation of knowledge and experience, and then living long enough to reflect on it, make sense of it, and apply it to oneself and others. Like Maslow, Sheehy believes that age and wisdom may not necessarily be connected, but that one (age) is a *necessary condition* for the achievement of the other (wisdom). Neither Sheehy nor Maslow is suggesting that "younger people" cannot be smart, intelligent, or clever, but rather that wisdom and insight require time and fermentation to develop.

Because of all of this, Sheehy advocates that we never completely retire, but rather, that we redirect our time, energy, and experience to actions, causes, and issues that simultaneously take us out of ourselves and give us an internal focus. For Sheehy, part of the task of our second adulthood is to find a worthy challenge. Something that will allow us to wear ourselves out, and not just rust-out! A task that will give truth to Tennyson's statement that it is never too late to "shine in use."[27]

When MarkTwain said, "Age is a matter of the mind, and if you don't mind, it doesn't matter," he wasn't absolutely correct, but he was on to something. Given certain variables, the fact is, age is as much about consciousness as it is about chronology. After all, "age" or "aging" is an arbitrary nomenclature, a variable that is subject to the widest cultural interpretations.[28] For example, all of us know people who were young at heart well into their nineties, and others who were cranky oldsters in their teens. My own mother once called me "the oldest, crabbiest man she had ever met." She did it at my eighth birthday party right after I criticized the quality of the decorations and the party favors—think *Frasier*!

When you think about it objectively, why is "old age" automatically a curse, and "youth" always a blessing? Every age has its crises. Every age has its problems. Every age has its highs and lows. Personally, I believe that thirteen to thirty are the toughest years of all. Think about it.

- The end of childhood
- Puberty
- Schooling
- The pursuit of identity
- Sex
- Adult status
- Marriage
- Kids of your own
- Mortgages
- Jobs and careers

A heavy load indeed, and all in a very compacted period of time.

And, let's not kid ourselves, the middle years—thirty to sixty—the supposed "golden years," aren't necessarily all that glorious either.

- First marriage ends.
- Second marriage, second set of kids, second set of in-laws.

- Kids grow up.
- Tuition payments.
- Second marriage ends (optional).
- Friends move.
- Your place and value in job market change.
- Your body begins to remind you that life is a cumulative injury disease.
- The kids come back.
- Parents die.
- Friends begin to die.
- Kids marry.
- A lot of stuff you used to think was fun isn't fun anymore.
- Kids move back with their kids.

Why can't "old age," our "second adulthood," sixty years and counting, be a time when—liberated from the pressures and hang-ups of a youth-oriented society driven by work, status, and success—we find relish in existence and search for a deeper meaning for life? Why can't maturity represent the highest point in human development? Why can't "old age" be our "Sabbath days"?

> In the passage in Exodus 31:17 [on the Sabbath], God rests and is refreshed. What God does is paradigmatic for us. Resting, in that passage, signifies cessation from work; being refreshed refers to activity that is creative and active and yields a sense of renewal and inspiration. Ceasing to work does not mean becoming idle or aimless. With leisure comes the opportunity for another kind of activity, the goal of which is the cultivation of one's soul and its potentialities.[29]

Of course, the quality of our second adulthood is dependent upon a number of critical variables, which include good physical and psychological health, financial independence, and a supportive network of family and friends. According to a recent study on adult development and injury by the Harvard Medical School, the secret to a long, happy life is dependent on seven major factors.

1. Not smoking or quitting early.
2. A positive mental attitude; being able to cope with, if not cure, life problems.
3. Not total abstinence from alcohol (thank God!), but the absence of alcohol abuse.
4. Healthy weight.
5. A solid marriage. (Ironically, after 30 years of a 50 percent divorce rate in first marriages, we now have proof that marriage is good for us!)
6. Exercise and physical activity. (And remember, sex is exercise too!)
7. Years of education. The more years of schooling people have, the more they tend to age successfully.

The study director, Dr. George E. Vaillant, claims that of the 24 men and women who had been tested and followed from their teens into their eighties, that individuals who had four or more of these seven factors at age fifty were one-third less likely to be dead by eighty. Individuals who had three or fewer of these factors at fifty—even though they were in good physical shape—were three times as likely to die during the following thirty years.[31]

Why, then, if we are lucky enough to possess four out of the seven variables, is it not possible for our second adulthood to be liberating rather than delimiting? Why can't the perspective of age allow us:

• To overcome our fear of irrelevance.
• To let go of our fear of failure.
• To let go of the tyranny of the dream, the tyranny of false expectations.

- To pack away illusion, false hopes, excessive desires.
- To see that we are not in this alone.

Why can't we see age as healthy growth, as a part of the conti-
nuity of life, as an opportunity for wisdom, and not simply as
the vestibule to death?

Age and aging are basic facts of life. The psychologist
Seymour Littallek warns that we have a personal duty and social
obligation to respect and honor the concepts of age and aging
in regard to both ourselves and others.

> A society that does not provide sufficient gratifications for the
> elderly will be an unhappy society for the young as well as the
> old. If the old are not gratified, nobody can accept the prospects
> of age with equanimity . . . for any society which cannot treat
> its elderly members decently is doomed to unremitting despair
> and chaos.[31]

epilogue

Sabbath as Metaphor

The average person is only capable of four productive hours of
work a day. The rest is spent filling time. Society often demands
more of a man's nature than he can give.

—*Thorne Lee*

Most of us have a confusing and complicated love-hate rela-
tionship with that ubiquitous state of being and four-letter
word: work! I, myself, am a workaholic. I didn't start off being
a workaholic. I started, according to the good nuns who taught
me in grammar school, as an overachiever and worked my way
up from there (pun intended). In graduate school, I was a
workaholic because I had to be, everyone else was so much
smarter than me. As a young professor, I was a workaholic
because the tenure clock was ticking and I had five years to produce a book based on original research or eight articles published in major journals. In my midthirties into my forties I was
a workaholic because I was unhappy in my personal life and my
work at least gave me focus and purpose. In my midforties, I
was a workaholic because of the creative joy and pleasure of the
work itself. I couldn't teach enough classes, see enough students, give enough public lectures, read enough, or write

enough to satisfy my passion and interest in my subject matter and work. Finally, I remain a workaholic primarily out of habit, and, secondarily, because a modicum of success has led me to injudiciously overextend myself and take on too many tasks. The point is, good excuse, bad excuse, no excuse at all—it's so easy to fall into the habits and patterns of being a workaholic.

According to Robert Reich, both the system and the psyche are stacked against us. Yes, we work for "addicted organizations." Yes, the competition of the global marketplace is palpably real. Yes, our information technology is blurring the line between our private and professional lives. Yes, we seek and desire lifestyles we are hard-pressed to financially maintain. And yet, Reich suggests, although we are driven by circumstance and technology, we are also driven by who we are. Our "call to endless work" seems to be about something in our genes, something that allows us to find gratification in responding to the "call of endless effort," without calling it quits.[1] (According to the United Nations Labor Organization in a 2001 report, Americans are putting in nearly fifty hours per week and 49.5 weeks a year on the job.)[2]

Although poets and songwriters would have us believe that love is the glue that holds the world together, they are wrong, says Mary Schmich, a *Chicago Tribune* columnist. At least half of the glue, she says, isn't love but work. "The world carries on in a semblance of order and goodwill because of what we all give to each other through what we make and do, even on the days when we don't want to do it, even when no one bothers to say thank you."[3]

Another newspaper columnist, Fred Moody of the *Baltimore City Paper*, agrees with both Reich's and Schmich's conclusions, but for slightly different reasons. Overworking is a long-recognized American trait, says Moody, and recently it has become the "signature of strenuous yuppies" who put in long hours while simultaneously complaining that their main problem in life is "lack of leisure time." Sadly, reports Moody, the career has taken precedence over such time-honored human endeavors as building a strong family or seeking spiritual and philosophical truths. The simple fact is "the person who works right up to the point of self-destruction is often accorded far more esteem than the person who seeks to lead a more balanced life." Moody believes the widespread pressure to work—at the expense of our physical health and the health of our relationships—has reached alarming dimensions. "I don't really want to put in 80 hour weeks," says one engineer who often does, "but a lot of people do. And those are the people who get the projects and promotions."[4]

The philosopher Bob Solomon, a world-class workaholic in his own right, would never argue that we are literally "hard wired to over work." But he would strongly argue that it is "*not in our nature not* to be active." One of the medieval definitions of humankind is *ratio animalis*, the rational animal. Today, anthropologists use the term *homo sapiens, sapiens*, the thinking and knowing hominoid, to define humans as a species. Another medieval definition of humanity is *homo faber*, man the doer, man the maker. For Solomon, perhaps the definition of choice should be *ago, ergo sum*, I act, therefore I am. We are restless by nature, says Solomon. We are doers. We are meant to be busy. Leisure, he contends, is not a natural condition. To do "nothing" is to deny our talents and temperament.

For Solomon, metaphorically speaking, it is but a "small evolutionary step" from being busy, to busy-ness, to the world of business and work. *Ago, ergo sum*; we are known to ourselves and others by what we do. And we are measured by others by our accomplishments. That's why, Solomon suggests, business is a good game: lots of action, a minimum of rules, and you keep score (at least partially) with money. In the long run, winding up a workaholic, says Solomon, is a matter of taste and circumstance. But whether we are known as an addict or lazy, we are all measured by the same yardstick, our "busy-ness quotient." We achieve identity through our actions.[5]

When you think about it, Solomon's "busy-ness thesis" goes a long way to explain why workaholics on the job usually wind up being workaholics off the job as well. As I've indicated earlier, workaholics are addicted to action; and this addiction does not suddenly stop when the five o'clock whistle blows. It's been my experience—as both an observer and a fellow addict—that workaholics do everything hard. They—okay, we—lack boundaries. We approach everything as a chore, a task, a duty, an obstacle to overcome, an accomplishment to be achieved, a competition to be entered and won. In its most optimistic light, we make everything a game, a contest to be won. In its most negative sense, we make everything a challenge, a direct threat to our sense of identity and self-worth. In either case, the strategy and tactics are the same: outdo your opponent and overwhelm the objective with energy and hustle. (I recently learned that in Chinese, the pictograph for the word "busy" is composed of two characters: *heart* and *killing*. Hmm! Interesting, don't you agree?)[6]

There is one other aspect of workaholism that both troubles me and causes me a great deal of personal guilt as a concerned parent. Because I was so busy doing "stuff," I overlooked the obvious: workaholism is a socially communicable disease. Anthropologists have long argued that both boys and girls learn their place and purpose in a community through the example and witness of others. Gender roles, rules, and duties as well as cultural standards, patterns, and expectations are not innate or intuitive but, rather, witnessed, learned, reinforced, and acquired. As standards change, so too do the models, reinforcement patterns, and rules of socialization. For example, in today's world both little boys and little girls want to grow up to be "firemen," "policemen," "teachers," and "priests." And just as very few boys want to grow up to be only a daddy, fewer and fewer little girls only want to be mommies. Work addiction, like other cultural phenomena, may be a generational disease. Families that are always doing things very often produce children who primarily value only what they do. (Aside to my children: Sorry about that, kids!)

Given this thesis of "busy-ness," let's go back and reexamine the topic of vacations. When a lot of us stop working, when we go off on vacation, we don't necessarily want to rest (as in relax and recover) or recreate (as in re-creating and re-forming ourselves); rather, we want to be stimulated, titillated, and entertained. Because our lives are so busy, says Daniel Boorstin in his influential text *The Image: A Guide to Pseudo-Events in America*, because our days are so project packed, because time is of the essence, "we want our two week vacations to be romantic, exotic, cheap, and effortless."[7] Moreover, it goes without saying, we also want them to be fun, fun, fun!

As the theologian Wayne Mullen points out, it now seems hopelessly archaic to suggest that you could have a good summer vacation by doing pretty much nothing at all. Long gone, says Mullen, are the lazy, languid weeks of summer, the hot days and warm nights sitting on the front porch, taking a walk, going on a simple picnic, or putting together a pickup game of baseball at the park. Instead, we buy ourselves "new and improved totally great summers" full of gadgets and toys like Jet Skis, roller blades, and mountain bikes and preplanned, prepackaged trips to Disneyland, Vegas, and/or Katmandu, Nepal.[8] Being "addicted to action" in our working lives, we seek the same nonstop pace off the job as well. Perhaps the only thing rivaling our almost infinite appetite for work, to use Aldous Huxley's handsome phrase, is our "almost infinite appetite for distractions."

Paying for leisure, paying for pleasure, paying for a good time, is a practice that long pre-dates us as a people and a nation. In fact, the exchange of lucre for pleasure goes back to time immemorial. Even the very word *lucre*, money, comes from the Greek *apolahein*, meaning enjoyment. The pleasures of travel—entertainment, gambling, food, alcohol, and recreational sex (brothels or a shipboard romance)—are not, after all, inventions of the late twentieth century. Roman historians are quick to point out that the sister cities of Pompeii and Herculaneum in southern Italy specialized in every possible form of pleasure for pay and are, in fact, the undeniable great-great-great-grandparents of modern-day Vegas and Reno. As a society, we are more than happy to pay top dollar for what we want, when we want it. The notion of quid pro quo is an ingrained part of our character. "If you've got it and we want it, we'll pay for it." After all, what's capitalism all about?

Although the selling of pleasure may not have begun on these shores, the wholesale commercialization of leisure to a mass audience is, it can be argued, a product of American ingenuity. Modern American examples include amusement parks, athletic complexes, gambling casinos, shopping malls, and cinema complexes. Even forms of leisure that were not originally commercially produced are now better able to sustain themselves because of commercialization. Museums, galleries, and national parks, for example, advertise themselves as destinations of choice, charge substantial fees for entrance, and significantly subsidize themselves through the sale of gifts and mementos in their authorized stores. And, of course, the examples par excellence of the commercialization of leisure are Las Vegas and Disneyland/Disney World.

Las Vegas, like Oz, is a figment of our collective imagination and ingenuity. It is a city in the desert of Nevada that lacks an adequate or readily available supply of energy or water. It is not a center for agriculture or animal husbandry, nor does its geographical location qualify it as a hub of commerce or transportation. The only reasons for the development and growth of Las Vegas were Nevada's lax laws in regard to gambling and liquor licensing, the availability of cheap parcels of land, and the vision and risk taking of a Jewish "accounting Don" from the New York Mafia in the early 1940s, Bugsy Siegel.

Las Vegas today is like a giant birthday cake in the middle of the desert. Its glow can be seen by orbiting shuttle flights, and it is recognized as the modern Mecca of adult entertainment and gambling. One of the most striking features of the city is the rapid rate at which it reinvents itself. Hotels and casinos are routinely demolished in order to build bigger, more elaborate ones. This is done not because the older hotels are decrepit, but because the city believes it must continuously offer new venues, motifs, and themes that are ever more spectacular in order to keep tourists interested and eager to vacation there. For example, in order to attract parents with children, "family friendly" hotels with mini-theme parks whose services include day care facilities and nighttime baby-sitters—so the kids can play and be secure while mom and dad are free to golf, gamble, dine, and dance—sprouted up along "the strip."

After Disney's initial success in Anaheim, California, Walt and company decided to make the "Mickey experience" bicoastal and purchased a huge parcel of undeveloped land near Orlando, Florida. Disney World is Disneyland on serious steroids. It's larger in scope, scale, and facilities, and is more dispersed and capable of accommodating many more "guests" than its Californian soul mate. Like Vegas, the building of Disney World occurred from scratch and required totally reshaping the Floridian hinterland by the draining of swamps, the creation of an interstate highway system, and the development of quotidian necessities such as power, water, and sewage.

I'm only a little embarrassed to admit that I have visited and enjoyed many, if not all, of the delights offered by Vegas and the dual Disneys on a number of occasions. While none of these locations would make my top ten list of vacation spots, nor are they locales I'd eagerly choose to revisit, I was not entirely unmoved by the fantasy, pleasure, and fun they had to offer. I can fully appreciate why Vegas and the Disneys can boast of being the "playlands" of America and the vacation spots of choice for most American families.

My problem, therefore, is not with slot machines and

showgirls or Mickey and Minnie per se; it is with what the dual Disneys and Vegas represent: the complete preplanned, prepackaged, often prepaid, commercialization of leisure. Although I do not consider all forms of such commercialization inherently bad and absolutely to be avoided, I do worry about the extent to which commercialized forms of leisure, entertainment, and diversions are displacing other kinds of leisure activities and enjoyments.[9]

The ethicist Richard Lippke agrees with me. Although Lippke argues that there doesn't seem to be any one best way to live out one's life or enjoy one's leisure, he believes that the continuous expansion of the commercialization of leisure can lead to the diminishment rather than the development of self. He contends that this trend should give us pause in five areas.

1. Lack of Self Development. Leisure time is time when individuals might independently cultivate knowledge, interests, skills, and sensitivities that enable them to participate in new and different activities that they find enjoyable. Commercial forms of leisure such as television, movies, music concerts, and spectator sports tend to make their audiences passive participants in their own enjoyment. Rather than actually doing or creating things, individuals sit back and watch others do things.

2. Lack of Autonomy. Whatever else it might be, leisure time is, in principle, time away from the controlling authority of business enterprises and the demands and dictates of others. Commercial forms of leisure tend to undermine the abilities and dispositions needed if individuals are to function autonomously, and thus direct their lives in a reflective and independent fashion.

3. Effects on Social Life. Many commercial forms of leisure seem to promote shallow social relations instead of requiring or encouraging individuals to interact with one another in ways that involve discussion, negotiation, planning, arguing, working together, and compromising. Commercial forms of leisure increasingly lead individuals to engage in what might be called "parallel spectatorship." People may enjoy some form of leisure activity in close proximity to others, but their interaction with others is both minimal and fairly passive.

4. Positional Competition. Positional competition is fostered by marketing techniques that tell individuals they will be judged negatively by their peers if they do not purchase or own the most up-to-date or sophisticated consumer products. As positional competition techniques are utilized in the prepackaged leisure industry, social status is increasingly being measured by where and how individuals go on vacation.

5. Cognitive and Valuational Confusion. Purveyors of commercialized leisure depict the social worlds at exotic vacation spots as exciting, fast paced, and romantic. They promise thrills, opportunities and pleasure at every turn. They purposefully create unrealistic and unrealizable standards. In so doing they breed constant disenchantenment and disillusionment with our normal lives.[10]

Having said all of this, I am still more than a little sympathetic to the enticing siren calls and promises of comfort and delight to be had in selecting or settling for a prepackaged vacation. We all feel that we work long and hard. Most of us get very limited time off from the job. And when we do, we want to do something different, something special. We want an interesting interlude. We want to escape the tyranny and tedium of the everyday. We want to have fun, and we don't want to have to work at planning or preparing for it either. We already do enough work. So why not just pay, pack, and play? It makes perfect sense to a lot of people.

Hey, when you think about it, few things in life are purely

serendipitous. Most things have to be planned for. And more often than not, the better the plan, the better the outcome. But sometimes, who's got time to plan? So why not deal with somebody who knows what they're doing? They plan, you play. Nothing could be easier. Although writing a check is not the same thing as long hours studying Michelin guide books, I guarantee you that it will get you to where you want to go!

To tell you the truth, no matter my addiction to work, I love to travel. I love to go on vacation. And, over the years I have traveled both first-class and third-, on the promenade deck and in steerage, and by means of a Mercedes as well as a motor scooter. Frankly, to paraphrase the words of the songstress Sophie Tucker, I've traveled rich and I've traveled poor. Rich is much better! Nevertheless, both methods of travel have their benefits as well as drawbacks and both can prove to be a meaningful way of discovering the pleasures and the wonders of the world around us.

My problem is not with what we do on vacations, or where we go on vacations, or how much we spend on vacations. My problem revolves around the issue of what most of us *don't get* out of our vacations—the opportunity for solitude and Sabbath.

As a culture whose mythology is steeped in the hard work and accomplishment of our pioneering forebears, we just *don't do nothing well!* We are not known as a nation of relaxers! Despite the mythology of the '60s, we are not a laid-back group. We rarely deliberately devote ourselves to idleness. Although I know it sounds like a Zen paradox, we almost never slow down enough to experience the experience of *not doing anything at all.* We just don't do leisure well. We rarely attune our inner ear to the needs of our inner self. We usually stay too busy. We usually do too much, and in the doing insulate ourselves from ourselves. As a friend once told me: "Most of us will take time off, but very few of us want to spend time with only ourselves. It's too boring and scary. It's a lot easier to do something and just keep busy."

In an almost completely forgotten book (again, who's got the leisure to read anymore?), *Solitude: A Return to the Self*, the English psychiatrist Anthony Storr speaks to a profoundly neglected human need: the need for solitude. The *Random House Dictionary* defines solitude as "the state of being or living alone." Although optimum solitude can occur only in the physical absence of others, the general state of solitude can be achieved in the presence of others. Just as it is possible to be lonely in the company of others, it is also possible to achieve solitude, of a kind, in the company of others.

The state of solitude is about calmness, centeredness, and focus. It's the ability to get "lost in the present." It's about being able to rivet our attention, getting in touch with our deepest thoughts and feelings. It's about being able to ruminate without distraction, to meditate, to idly muse, to become totally absorbed in thought.

Of course, a lonely mountaintop is always preferable, but solitude can be had about anywhere. The playwright David Mamet has said: "I like writing in restaurants. The noise and busyness forces me inside my head. I'm able to totally concentrate on what I'm doing." The novelist Scott Turow wrote his first best-selling novel, *Presumed Innocent*, over a period of eight years while commuting back and forth to work on public transportation. "Complete solitude," said Turow, "was a luxury, all I could afford was focus."

Anthony Storr argues that solitude is a pleasure, a virtue, and a human necessity. For Storr, part of our emotional and intellectual maturity is measured by our ability to achieve and cope with solitude. Solitude, says Storr, is linked to self-discovery and self-realization. It is both the catalyst and the conduit for change and creativity. Storr believes that no one will ever fully develop the capacities of their intellect without the solemnity and intellectual sanctuary provided by solitude.

One of the many paradoxes of the human condition is that although we need each other and learn from each other, we are

also distracted by the presence of others and kept from ourselves by others. Greta Garbo was psychologically profound and not just being "campy" when she demanded her right to privacy: "I want to be alone." All of us need to be alone. Solitude acts as our gyroscope and compass. We flounder or travel less well without it. Solitude, says Storr, allows us a respite from the distractions and distortions of the everyday world. Solitude gives us access to our own thoughts. It is a form of self-therapy. It allows us to hear ourselves think. It allows us to think out

loud to ourselves.[11] To paraphrase e. e. cummings: How do I
know what I really think, until I get a chance to hear what I have
to say? Perhaps Wordsworth summed it up best in *The Prelude*.

When from our better selves we have too long
Been parted by the hurrying world, and droop,
Sick of its business, of its pleasures tired,
How gracious, how benign, is Solitude.

Of course, achieving solitude is easier said than done. As
William James pointed out, reality is a "booming, buzzing, confusion." The excessive busyness of our multitasked lives and the
constant overload of outside stimuli are much more conducive
to the production of migraines than to the pursuit of meaning.
Nevertheless, suggests Storr, "finding down-time," "time outside of usual time," "time to reflect on time," is a sine qua non
condition for emotional and intellectual stability.

At the risk of sounding like a born-again something-or-
other or, worse yet, an acolyte of Leo Buscaglia, solitude can
offer us a window to our deepest selves—our psyches, our spir-
its, or, if you will, our souls. We need to take vacations, to vacate
ourselves from the everydayness of life if only for a while.
Vacations, long walks, quiet weekends, time alone, time to think
should not be considered a perk or a privilege but rather a
necessity of the human condition. We need not always be doing.
We must studiously do less in order to be more.

Freud has said that getting in touch with our deepest sense
of self is one of the most difficult things we can ever do. It
requires time, energy, effort, patience, and practice. And if and
when we achieve our objective, said Freud, the degree of diffi-
culty grows even higher. Insight now requires further reflection
and response. "Do I like this or that aspect of myself? Should I,
must I, can I, change it? Can I make it better? Can I make it go
away?" Because of all of this, suggested Freud, we flee from or

avoid solitude and reflection and seek distraction rather than insight, merriment rather than meaning.

In chapter 2 we briefly discussed the Sabbath as a formal religious ritual with rules, regulations, and requirements. I argued that the Sabbath, the day of rest, is a mandated time for reflection on the marvels and mysteries of life and a time to ponder the architecture and architect of time. I'd like now to turn to a more generic or secular understanding of Sabbath.

Wayne Muller, in his insightful and moving text *Sabbath*, argues that in the relentless busyness of modern life, we have lost the rhythm between work and rest. And because we do not rest enough, says Muller, we lose our way, and are often unsure about how to proceed.[12] Although the Sabbath is a specific religious practice, the concept of Sabbath, says Muller, is also a larger metaphor, a starting point to invoke a conversation about the necessity to rest. Like solitude, Sabbath is a way of creating a time where we can examine who we are and what we know, and reflect on what we have. Sabbath-like solitude is about letting go, being fallow, and looking within. Sabbath, says Muller, does not require us to "leave home, change jobs, go on retreat, or leave the world of ordinary life."[13] Nor do we have to change clothes or purchase any expensive equipment. But we do have to stop. Sabbath is about surrender, being open to other possibilities. Sabbath is a time when discipline should studiously be avoided. Sabbath is about stopping everything and taking time out before time runs out. Sabbath is refuge, a disconnect from the frenzy of work, consumption, and accomplishment.[14]

Muller argues that rest is an essential enzyme of life, a catalyst, as necessary as air or water. "Without rest, we cannot sustain the energy needed to have life."[15] Sadly, says Muller, in a world where overwork is considered a professional virtue, too many of us feel that we can be legitimately stopped only by physical illness or collapse. Illness then becomes our Sabbath. In other words, many of us give ourselves permission to back off only when a crisis occurs. Our pneumonia, our cancer, our heart attack, our accidents create rest for us. They give us permission to stop and reflect. Muller reminds us that "on the seventh day" even God found it necessary to rest.

Sabbath time is about "useless things" that only have value when we have the time to appreciate and do them.

> To walk without purpose, to no place in particular, where we are astonished by the textured bark of an oak. To notice the color red showing itself for the first time in the maple in fall. To see animals in the shapes of clouds, to walk in clover. To fall into an unexpected conversation with a stranger, and find something delicious and unbidden take shape. To taste the orange we eat, the juice on the chin, the pulp between teeth. To take a deep sigh, an exhale, followed by a listening silence. To allow a recollection of a moment with a loved one, a feeling of how our life has evolved. To give thanks for a single step upon earth. To give thanks for any blessing, previously unnoticed . . . the gentle brush of a hand on a lover's body, the sweet surrender of sleep in the afternoon.[16]

In my mind's eye, I can hear my mother now: "Talk, talk, talk! Theory, theory, theory! That's all you professor types do! Enough already! Stop already! Tell me something I can relate to. All this 'busyness' and 'sabbath as metaphor' you've been talking about. All this stuff we do and don't do. Tell me something real. Just give me two not twenty examples of what's changed or missing in our lives!" (You know, even if it's only happening inside my own head, my mother's words still scare the hell out of me!) Okay, mom, when you're right, you're right. So here are two examples that I know you'll be able to relate to: food and sleep.

The social theorist Bradley K. Googins has pointed out that how, what, and when we eat as families and as individuals has undergone a sea change since World War II. In the 1950s, the model family, even if it was only a short-lived and certainly not a universal experience, had a mom at home taking care of the children and chores and a dad at work. Googins conjectures that because mom was at home and, most probably, so was a widowed grandmother, and fast foods were as yet a thing of the future, most dinners were prepared at home and families ate out approximately three times a year. In the 1990s, however, says Googins, with both parents working and grandma in an extended-care facility, fast foods and preprocessed meals dominate as home cuisine and most families eat out on average three times a week.[17]

According to James R. Lencioni of The Aria Group, a nationally known architecture firm that specializes in restaurant design, the rule of thumb in the industry is that working individuals—single or married, with or without children—spend approximately 25 percent of their distributive income on eating out or ordering out. However, this does not necessarily mean a steady diet of luxurious meals at Chateau Poulet. More realistically, for most of us, what it means is picking up a bucket of chicken at Café Popeye's at the local strip mall.

If a former high-ranking executive at McDonald's is to be believed (it was, after all, New Year's Eve, it was late, and, clearly, he was not the designated driver for his family that evening), the Golden Arches is the most frequented restaurant chain in America, if not the world. Worldwide, with 28,000 restaurants in 121 different countries, McDonald's serves 45 million people every day. There are approximately 12,804 McDonald's in America, and one out of every seven Americans has at least one meal a week at a McDonald's restaurant. According to the Utne Reader, fast-food restaurants of all kinds account for 50 percent of all food eaten away from home in the United States and 25 perceent of all food eaten away from home in Europe. The only European exception to this rule is Italy, where fast-food intake hovers at 5 percent.[18]

The issue here is not simply the health and gastronomical

differences between the preparation and enjoyment of home-cooked cuisine versus fast-food takeouts, although that's clearly a part of it. The issue is, at least for me, that we haven't just lost or given up on the "art of cooking," but that we've also lost our taste for the "art of eating together."

Growing up in my mother's and grandmother's kitchen, I learned early on that food was sacred, preparing food was a holy rite, and eating together a religious statement of familial piety! During the week there was, of course, some flexibility, but we nevertheless ate most of our meals together Mondays through Saturdays. Sunday, however, was a "double holy day of obligation." That is, according to the Catholic Church, missing mass on Sunday was a mortal sin, and, according to my father, missing dinner at 1:30 P.M. on Sunday was an equally heinous offense. Except for illness, dismemberment, or death, eating together on Sunday was mandatory. (Church, by the way, was only one hour long, dinner could be dragged out for two to three hours!)

Yes, times were different. Yes, there were different rules in place. Yes, there was less to do and less to be distracted by. And yes, some of those Sunday meals were torturously boring and repetitious. But at their core, they were a statement and a ritual of well-earned rest, celebration, and thanks. They were about sharing and caring for others that you were related to by law or blood. It was my father saying: "I love you and I work hard to prove that every day. My labor has paid for the bounty of this table. Enjoy and show respect!" It was my mother saying: "I love you and I've worked hard to prepare this meal for you. Enjoy and be grateful for all that we have! *Mange, mange e fatte grosso. Fae Contento!*"

Today there is a movement, which not so surprisingly started in Italy, that is just beginning to have an impact in the United States. It's called *mange piano*—"eat slowly" or, more idiomatically, "slow food." The Italian "slow food" movement is literally saying: *Fermata! Basta!* "Stop!" "Enough!" We've all been

McMuffinized to death! We've lost the pleasure of eating in regard to both taste and togetherness.[19]

The "slow food" movement is not just about flavor, freshness, and nutritional value. It's not just a rebellion against convenience products and homogenization. Fundamentally, it's about the primal experience of breaking bread with family and friends. It is a bonding and learning experience, says Leon R. Kass, author of *The Hungry Soul*, that has huge implications for the individual and the society at large. For Kass, the equation is a basic one: A civil society starts at the family table with a civil meal.

> True, fast food, TV dinners, and eating on the run save time, meet our need for "fuel" and provide close to instant gratification. But for these very reasons, they diminish opportunities for conversation, communion, and sensuous pleasure; they thus shortchange the hungers of the soul. Meals eaten in front of the television set turn eating into feeding. Wolfing down food dishonors both the human effort to prepare it and the lives of plants and animals sacrificed on our behalf. The habits of incivility, insensitivity, and ingratitude learned at the family dinner table are carried out in the wider world, infecting all of American life.[20]

The other example I want to offer is just as basic and necessary as food; it's sleep. In a 1995 cover story *Newsweek* reported that 25 percent of us say we're fried by our work, frazzled by the lack of time, and just plain exhausted.[21] Arlie Russell Hochschild suggests that our lives and schedules are so exhausting that too many of us talk about sleep in the same longing way that hungry people talk about food.[22] Symptoms of exhaustion and fatigue are now among the top five reasons why people consult with their doctors. Although physicians are quick to point out that "exhaustion" is an umbrella term and not a medical term or a diagnosis, fatigue symptoms can herald any number of serious illnesses. (However, chronic fatigue syndrome, also called Epstein-Barr and Yuppie's Disease, is very rare, affecting only 5 percent of those who suffer long-term fatigue). Dr. Sheldon Miller, chair of psychology at Northwestern University, says that exhaustion is the body crying out "I've had it."[23]

According to a survey conducted in 2001 by the National Sleep Foundation, our workaholic lifestyle is turning America into a "nodding off nation," with 40 percent of those surveyed reporting difficulties staying awake during the day and on the job. The poll reported that although people need between seven and ten hours of sleep each night, 62 percent of those surveyed sleep less than eight hours per night. And of those sleeping less than eight hours 31 percent reported sleeping seven hours, and 31 percent sleep six hours or less per night. And 38 percent of all those surveyed said they sleep less now than they did five years ago and suffer from mild to chronic bouts of insomnia and sleep apnea.[24] (Maybe all of this helps to explain the phenomenal success of Starbucks. Their name has become synonymous with coffee; its stock has been on a steady growth pattern for years; and it can't keep up with the demand for new franchises. Soon there may be a Starbucks on every street corner in America. And, all of them will be jammed with people clamoring for a grande, a vente, or a double latte. I think, however, that the real secret to Starbucks' success isn't so much its coffee as the caffeine, and our need to stay awake!)

If you're like most people, you know that a sleepless night can zap your energy and turn your brain to mush. Well, says Eve Van Cauter, professor of medicine and sleep research at the University of Chicago, that's just the beginning of your problems when you chronically miss too much sleep. Because sleep serves so many purposes, says Dr. Van Cauter, not getting enough of it appears to have wide-ranging effects on our health. "We need sleep for almost everything," she says. "Studies are beginning to show that no matter what system you look at—whether it's memory, learning, the immune system, endocrine system, or sugar metabolism—when you look at those systems in subjects who are sleep deprived on a chronic basis, you find exaggerated negative effects." Sleep researchers are now in general agreement that chronic lack of sleep may be as bad for a person's health as smoking, a poor diet, and a lack of exercise. We need sleep, says Van Cauter, to rest and build our brains, to heal, to clear our cobwebs, to slow aging and dementia, and to help avoid obesity, diabetes, and hypertension.[25]

So, mama, what do you think? Aren't food and sleep pretty good examples? Don't they nicely illustrate the metaphor of Sabbath—as time out, time away from the usual, a time to rest, take a nap, or play?

Our society has grown to expect more and more from us and in less time; and, to an extent, we each bear some responsibility for allowing this to happen. Because we are so busy, we forget that working hard does not mean that we're making anything happen that matters or makes a difference to anyone, including ourselves.

A life of all work, or all play, or all rest would not be a balanced one. The Book of Ecclesiastes is not wrong. For everything there is a season and a time for every matter under heaven—a time to be born, to grow, to learn, to love, to work, to play, to rest, to be thankful—then, I think, the dying part will be much easier to bear. The trick is to get the ingredients and the proportions balanced and right. Frankly, it's no simple task.

I'd write more, but I've worked enough on this project. So, I'm actually going to practice what I preach. I'm going to have something to eat, take a nap, tell my wife and children that I love them, and then we're going on vacation. Italy anyone? Ciao!

Notes

Prologue

1. Wayne Muller, *Sabbath* (New York: Bantam Books, 1999), 2, 3.
2. John Robinson and Geoffrey Godbey, *Time for Life: The Surprising Way Americans Use Their Time* (University Park: Pennsylvania State University Press, 1997). Richard Wronski, "Time Warped," *Chicago Tribune*, June 15, 1997, Perspective Section, 1, 4.
3. Marc Peyser, "Time Bind? What Time Bind?," *Newsweek*, May 12, 1997, 69.
4. James Gleick, *Faster* (New York: Pantheon Books, 1999), 12.
5. Ibid., 277.
6. Benjamin Kline Hunnicut, "A Fast-Paced Look at the Whirl and Flux of Modern Life," *Chicago Tribune*, September 19, 1999, Books, 8.
7. Jacqueline Fitzgerald, "Partners 9–5 and Beyond," *Chicago Tribune*, April 11, 2001, Women Section, 2.
8. Mark Harris, "The Game of Life," *Utne Reader*, March–April 2001, 61, 62.
9. Steven Greenhouse, "In U.S., Workers Toil Even Longer," *Chicago Tribune*, September 1, 2001, 1.
10. Joe Robinson, "Four Weeks Vacation for Everyone!," *Utne Reader*, September–October 2000, 49, 50.
11. Sue Shellenbarger, "Canceling a Vacation Could Cost You Dearly in the Long Run," *Wall Street Journal*, April 16, 2001, 8.
12. Harris, "The Game of Life," 61, 62.
13. Wayne Booth, *For the Love of It* (Chicago: University of Chicago Press, 1999), 174.
14. William Neikirk, "Jobless Claims Jump, Dashing Rebound Hopes," *Chicago Tribune*, December 14, 2001, 1.

15. Martin Crutsinger, "Sales Drop, but So Do Jobless Claims," *Chicago Sun-Times*, December 14, 2001, 65.

16. Dableen Glanton, "September 11 a Hard Blow to Florida," *Chicago Tribune*, January 1, 2002, Section I, 10; Glanton, "It's a Goofy World, Mick," *Chicago Tribune*, October 31, 2001, Working, 1.

17. Shellenbarger, "In Cataclysmic Times, Workers Need Room to Rethink Priorities," *Wall Street Journal*, December 12, 2001, 8.

Chapter I

1. Julia Keller, "Help Wanted: Must Be Laid-Back, Fun-Loving, Presidential," *Chicago Tribune*, March 29, 2001, Tempo Section, 1.

2. T. Sullivan and A.Gini, *Heigh-Ho! Heigh-Ho!—Quotes about Work* (Chicago: ACTA Press, 1994), 109.

3. Josef Pieper, *Leisure: The Basis of Culture* (New York: New American Library, 1963), 50.

4. Arlie Russell Hochschild, *The Second Shift* (New York: Viking, 1989), 9.

5. Juliet B. Schor, *The Overworked American* (New York: Basic Books, 1991), 30, 31.

6. Charles Hardy, *The Age of Paradox* (Boston: Harvard Business School Press, 1994), 29, 30.

7. Thomas Geoghegan, "The Role of Labor," *Baumhart Business Ethics Lectures*, Loyola University Chicago, May 4, 1996.

8. Hochschild, *The Time Bind* (New York: Metropolitan Books, 1997), 26.

9. Daniel H. Pink, *Free Agent Nation* (New York: Time Warner, 2001), 104.

10. "Workforce Trends," *Spotlight: Journal of Career Planning and Employment*, January 18, 1994, 1.

11. T. Shawn Taylor, Work Buzz, "Feeling Overworked: When Work Becomes Too Much," *Chicago Tribune*, June 13, 2001, Section 6, 1.

12. Mike Royko, "Silver Spoon Fits, Why Not Wear It?" *Chicago Tribune*, November 11, 1985, Section 1, 3.

13. Pink, *Free Agent Nation*, 105.

14. Philip Larkin, "Toads," in *The Less Deceived* (Plymouth, England: Marvell Press, 1978), 28, 29. Reprinted by permission of The Marvell Press, England and Australia.

15. Deborah Baldwin, "As Busy as We Wanna Be," *Utne Reader*, January–February 1994, 54.

16. Quoted in ibid., 54.

17. Ibid., 56.

18. Ibid., 55.

19. Diane Fassel, *Working Ourselves to Death* (San Francisco: Harper San Francisco, 1990), 28, 29, 30.

20. Ibid., 3.

21. Ibid., viii, (parentheses added).

22. Ibid., 72.

23. Ibid., 4.

24. Ibid., 16.

25. Ibid., 109.

26. T. Shawn Taylor, Work Buzz, "Vanishing Vacation—All Work, No Play," *Chicago Tribune*, February 28, 2001, Section 6, 1.

27. "Vacation Please: Requests Pile Up as Summer Looms," *Wall Street Journal*, May 8, 2001, 1.

28. Steve Lopez, Santa Monica, "What You Need Is More Vacation!," *Time*, June 12, 2000, 8.

29. Ibid.

30. Schor, *The Overworked American*, 23, 24.

31. Nancy Gibbs, "How America Has Run Out of Time," *Time*, April 24, 1989, 59.

Chapter 2

1. Anna Quindlen, "Happy Leader, Happy Nation," *Newsweek*, January 15, 2001, 64.

2. Quindlen, *A Short Guide to a Happy Life* (New York: Random House, 2000), 16.

3. Robert B. Reich, *The Future of Success* (New York: Alfred A. Knopf, 2001), 217.

4. Witold Rybczynski, *Waiting For the Weekend* (New York: Viking, 1991), 224.

5. Wayne E. Oates, *Workaholics, Make Lazyness Work for You* (Garden City, N.Y.: Doubleday and Company, 1978), 3, 4.

6. Ibid., 4.

7. Ibid., 47, 48.

8. Hannah Arendt, *The Human Condition* (New York: Doubleday Anchor Books, 1959), 111.

9. Diane Ackerman, *Deep Play* (New York: Random House, 1999), 6.

10. Donald Hall, *Life Work* (Boston: Beacon Press, 1993), 23.

11. Erich Fromm, *The Sane Society* (Greenwich, Conn.: Fawcett Publications, 1955), 253.

12. Rybczynski, *Waiting For the Weekend*, 15.

13. Leonard Fagin, "Psychiatry (and Work)," in *Social Anthropology of Work*, Sandra Wallman, ed. (London: Academic Press, 1979), 33.

14. Rybczynski, *Waiting For the Weekend*, 16–19.

15. Ibid., 226.

16. Josef Pieper, *Leisure: The Basis of Culture* (New York: New American Library, 1963), 40–44.

17. Ibid., 27.

18. *Plutarch's Lives* (New York: Modern Library, 1932), 183.

19. Sar A. Levitan and Wm. B. Johnston, *Work Is Here to Stay, Alas* (Salt Lake City: Olympian Publishing, 1973), 28.

20. Rybczynski, *Waiting For the Weekend*, 51.

21. Oates, *Workaholics, Make Lazyness Work for You*, 48.

22. Ibid., 48, 49.

23. Matthew Fox, *The Reinvention of Work* (San Francisco: HarperCollins, 1994), 255–76.

24. Wayne Muller, *Sabbath* (New York: Bantam Books, 1999), 30.

25. Pieper, *Leisure: The Basis of Culture*, 37.

26. Ibid., 50.

Chapter 3

1. Charles Strum, "Family Driving: The New Model," *New York Times*, A Vacation Special Section, May 15, 2001, 1, 8.

2. Cindy S. Aron, *Working at Play* (New York: Oxford University Press, 1999), 2.

3. Sylvester Monroe, Andrea Sachs, and Elizabeth Taylor, "The New Face of America," *Time*–Special Edition, fall 1993, 65.

4. John Hilkevitch, "Pie in the Sky?" *Chicago Tribune*, August 12, 2001, Section 14, 1. "Morning Edition—NPR," WBEZ-FM Chicago, September 25, 2001.

5. Aron, *Working at Play*, 32, 33, 34.

6. John Winokur, ed., *The Portable Curmudgeon* (New York: NAL, 1987), 226.

7. Aron, *Working at Play*, 35, 36.

8. Ibid., 38.

9. Ibid., 39.

10. Ibid., 2, 3.

11. Ibid., 5.

12. Ibid., 197.

13. Ibid., 197. (Italics mine.)

14. Daniel J. Boorstin, *The Image* (New York: Atheneum, 1980), 77, 78.

15. Aron, *Working at Play*, 54.

16. Charles Strum, "Family Driving: The New Model," 1, 8.

17. Ibid.

18. Craig Ray, "Take It to the Limit," *Equinox: The Magazine of Southern South African Hotels*, June 2001, 59, 61.

19. Karl Taro Greenfield, "Life on the Edge," *Time*, September 6, 1999, 34, 36.

20. Quoted in ibid., 31.

21. George F. Will, "Bush's America Is Working," *Newsweek*, August 6, 2001, 64.

22. "Morning Edition—NPR," WBEZ-FM Chicago, August 5, 2001.

23. Garrison Keillor, "In Praise of Laziness," *Time*, September 10, 2001, 94.

24. Joe Robinson, "Four Weeks Vacation For Everyone!," *Utne Reader*, September-October 2000, 49–54.

25. Ibid., 50.

26. Bonnie Miller Rubin, "Vacation No Easy Getaways for Executives," *Chicago Tribune*, September 2, 2001, Section 5, 1, 5.

27. "848–With Steve Edwards," NPR, WBEZ-FM Chicago, September 5, 2001.

28. Bonnie Miller Rubin, "Vacation No Easy Getaways for Executives," 5.

29. Ibid.

30. Ibid.

Chapter 4

1. Juliet B. Schor, *The Overworked American* (New York: Basic Books, 1991), 10.

2. Witold Rybczynski, *Waiting For the Weekend* (New York: Viking Press, 1991), 52.

3. Schor, *The Overworked American*, 6.

4. Rybczynski, *Waiting For the Weekend*, 215.

5. Schor, *The Overworked American*, 46, 47.

6. Ibid., 6, 7.

7. Ibid., 43–48.

8. Ibid., 7.

9. Sandra Jones, "Homework: The Changing Workplace," *Crain's Chicago Business*, August 12, 2001, E-12.

10. Rybczynski, *Waiting For the Weekend*, 23, 24.

11. Ibid., 24–28.

12. Ibid., 30, 48, 49.

13. Ibid., 49.

14. Ibid., 142–47.

15. Schor, *The Overworked American*, 61, 62.

16. Rybczynski, *Waiting For the Weekend*, 142.

17. Ibid., 143, 144.

18. Ibid., 216.

19. Ibid., 144.

20. Ibid., 12.

21. Mark Caro, " 'Harry Potter' Is Magic at the Turnstiles," *Chicago Tribune*, November 19, 2001, Section 5, 1. David Germain, " 'Star Wars II' Grosses $116 Million," *Chicago Tribune*, May 20, 2002, Section 5, 3.

22. Gregg Zoroya, "Beachhouse Escapism, East Coast–Style," *USA Today*, July 5, 2001, Section D, 1, 2.

23. Mariott-Residence Inn ad, *USA Today*, July 6, 2001, Section D, 12.

24. Rybczynski, *Waiting For the Weekend*, 222.

25. Ibid., 22.

26. Ibid., 18, 19.

27. Ibid., 19.

Chapter 5

1. Juliet B. Schor, *The Overspent American* (New York: Basic Books, 1998), 4–24.

2. Michael Elliot, *The Day before Yesterday: Reconsidering America's Past, Rediscovering the Future* (New York: Simon and Schuster, 1996), 17.

3. Maxine Chernoff, *American Heaven* (Minneapolis: Coffee House Press, 1996), 158.

4. Elliot, *The Day Before Yesterday*, 21ff.

5. Schor, *The Overworked American* (New York: Basic Books, 1991), 2.

6. Daniel Bell, "Work and Its Discontents," in A. Gini and T. J. Sullivan, *It Comes With the Territory* (New York: Random House, 1989), 117.

7. William Greider, *One World Ready or Not* (New York: Simon and Schuster, 1997).

8. Herbert Marcuse, *One-Dimensional Man* (Boston: Beacon Press, 1964), 9, 79.

9. Erich Fromm, *To Have or To Be?* (New York: Harper and Row, 1976), 15, 16, 19, 26.

10. David A. Crocker, "Consumption and Well Being," *Philosophy and Public Policy* 15, 4 (fall 1995), 13.

11. Adam Smith, *The Wealth of Nations* (New York: Modern Library, 1937), 625.

12. John DeGraaf, David Wann, and Thomas H. Naylor, *Affluenza* (San Francisco: Berrett-Koehler, 2001), 13. Reprinted with permission of the publisher. © 2001 by John DeGraaf, David Wann, and Thomas H. Naylor. Berrett-Koehler Publishers, Inc., San Francisco, CA. All rights reserved. www.bkcommection.com.

13. Mary Ellen Podmolik, "Malls Aim to Amuse Families," *Chicago Sun-Times*, May 6, 1999, 54.

14. DeGraaf, Wann, and Naylor, *Affluenza*, 41.

15. Anna Quindlen, "Honestly—You Shouldn't Have," *Newsweek*, December 3, 2001, 76.

16. Schor, *The Overworked American*, 107–9.

17. Jon Anderson, "Shop Till You Drop," *Chicago Tribune*, July 15, 1994, Tempo Section, 1.

18. DeGraaf, Wann, and Naylor, *Affluenza*, 4, 13.

19. Schor, *The Overworked American*, 107, 108.

20. Amanda Vogt, "It's a Mall, Mall World," *Chicago Tribune*, April 8, 1997, Kids News Section, 1.

21. DeGraaf, Wann, and Naylor, *Affluenza*, 62.

22. Ibid., 16.

23. James Coates, "Expectations Ease for Business On-Line," *Chicago Tribune*, July 21, 1997, Business Section, 2.

24. Barbara Rose, "Weekly Web Sales Reach $600 Million," *Chicago Tribune*, December 10, 2001, 1. "E-commerce," *All Things Considered*, NPR, WBEZ-FM Chicago, December 20, 2001.

25. DeGraaf, Wann, and Naylor, *Affluenza*, 13.

26. From *The Price* by Arthur Miller. © 1968 by Arthur Miller and Ingeborg M. Miller, Trustee. Used by permission of Viking Penguin, a division of Penguin Group (USA) Inc.

27. Schor, *The Overspent American*, 27–42.

28. William Lazar, "Marketing's Changing Social Relationships," *Journal of Marketing* 33 (January 1969), 8.

29. Ibid., 6.

30. Richard W. Pollay, "The Distorted Mirror: Reflections on the

Unintended Consequences of Advertising," *Journal of Marketing* 50 (April 1986), 26.

31. Michael Jacobsen and Laura Ann Mazur, *Marketing Madness* (Boulder, Colo., 1995).

32. Wayne Muller, *Sabbath* (New York: Bantam Books, 1999), 135.

33. Ibid., 148–53.

35. "Domestic Advertising Spending by Medium," AdAge.com accessed on 4/1/2002.

36. DeGraaf, Wann, and Naylor, *Affluenza*, 3.

37. Ibid., 2.

38. Ibid., 105.

38. Quoted in Al Gini, *My Job My Self* (New York: Routledge, 2000), 150.

39. Ibid., 148.

40. William A. McDonough, "Waste Equals Food: Designing for Material and Ethical Prosperity," *Ruffin Lectures in Business Ethics: Environmental Challenges to Business*, Darden, University of Virginia, April 4–6, 1997, 43.

41. Matthew Fox, *The Reinvention of Work* (San Francisco: Harper, 1994), 7, 8.

Chapter 6

1. Christian K. Messenger, *Sports and the Spirit of Play in Contemporary American Fiction* (New York: Columbia University Press, 1990), 1.

2. Mariah Burton Nelson, *The Stronger Women Get, the More Men Love Football* (New York: Harcourt Brace and Co., 1994), 4–14.

3. *NSGA Industry Research and Statistics*, 1998 Sports Participation, www.nsga.org/guests/research/participation/partic2.html.

4. Neil Postman, "TV, Reading, and Kids: An Interview," *One Flight Up*, NPR, WBEZ-FM Chicago, June 18, 1992.

5. Mickey Rathbun, "The Essence of Sport," *Chicago Tribune*, March 29, 1998, Section 14, 19.

6. Nelson, *The Stronger Women Get, the More Men Love Football*, 22. T. Caplow, L. Hicks, and B. Wattenberg, *The First Measured Century* (Washington, D.C.: AEI Press, 2001), 121.

7. Caplow, Hicks, and Wattenberg, *The First Measured Century*, 120.

8. Wayne Friedman, "Super Bowl Ad Rates Fall for Second Year," September 4, 2001, AdAge.com. Bob Garfield, "Super Bowl Ads Score," September 29, 2001, Friedman, "3 Weeks to Go, but 20% of Super Bowl Ads Unsold," January 14, 2002, AdAge.com. Jim Kirk, "Super Bowl vs. Olympics," *Chicago Tribune*, January 31, 2002, Section 5, 1, 11. Nelson, *The Stronger Women Get, the More Men Love Football*. Rick Telander, *The Hundred Yard Lie* (New York: Simon and Schuster, 1989). Murray Sperder, *College Sports Inc.* (New York: Henry Holt, 1990). Robert D. Putnam, *Bowling Alone* (New York: Simon and Schuster, 2000). *U.S. Bureau of Statistics: Statistical Abstract of the United States*, 1996, 116th edition (Lanham, Md.: Bernaw Press, 1996), #415, #416, 260.

9. Patrick Fitzgerald, Sales Director, *One-on-One Sports Radio-Network*, 1935 Techny Rd., Northbrook, IL. 60062.

10. Bill Brashler, "Poor Athletes," *Chicago Tribune Magazine*, July 28, 1996, 13.

11. David Seideman, "Mantle Mania," *Chicago Tribune*, March 29, 1998, Section 14, 3.

12. Brashler, "Poor Athletes," 13, 14, 15.

13. Caplow, Hicks, and Wattenberg, *The First Measured Century*, 121.

14. Witold Rybczynski, *Waiting For the Weekend* (New York: Viking, 1991), 208.

15. Ibid., 198.

16. Gerald Early, ed., *Body Language: Writers on Sports* (St. Paul, Minn.: Graywolf Press, 1998), 20.

Chapter 7

1. Jeffrey Turner and Donald Helms, *Life Span Development* (Philadelphia: W.B. Sanders, 1979), 452.

2. Walli F. Leff and Marilyn G. Haft, *Time Without Work* (Boston: South End Press, 1983), 3–21.

3. Studs Terkel, *Working* (New York: Pantheon Books, 1974), xi.

4. Kathleen Parker, "Retirement for Some Just Isn't What It's Cracked Up to Be," *Chicago Tribune*, February 7, 2001, 19.

5. Robert B. Reich, *The Future of Success* (New York: Alfred A. Knopf, 2001), 114.

6. Leff and Haft, *Time Without Work*, 13.

7. Robert L. Kahn, *Work and Health* (New York: Wiley, 1981), 11.

8. David Gutmann, "Reclaiming Powers: Toward a New Psychology of Men and Women in Later Life" (New York: Basic Books, 1987).

9. Leff and Haft, *Time Without Work*, 5.

10. John Dewey, *Democracy in Education* (1916), Vol. 9 of *The Middle Works of John Dewey, 1899–1924* (Carbondale: Southern Illinois University Press, n.d.), 9.

11. Theodore Roszak, *Person/Planet* (New York: Anchor Books, 1979), 227.

12. Quoted in Terry Sullivan and Al Gini, *Heigh-Ho! Heigh-Ho!* (Chicago: ACTA Publications, 1994), 122.

13. Quoted in David Sharos, "Retiring Types? Hardly," *Chicago Tribune*, September 16, 2001, Section 6, 1, 7.

14. Pete Sheehan, "Back to Work," *Company*, spring 2001, 27, 28.

15. Sullivan and Gini, *Heigh Ho! Heigh Ho!*, 155.

16. David Mendell and Evan Osnos, "America Grows Older and a Lot Less Traditional," *Chicago Tribune*, May 15, 2001, 1, 14.

17. Daniel J. Levinson, *Seasons of a Man's Life* (New York: Alfred A. Knopf, 1978).

18. Gail Sheehy, *Understanding Men's Passages* (New York: Random House, 1998), 3–16.

19. Esther Pan and Elizabeth Roberts, "Home of the Grey," *Newsweek*, March 1, 1999, 50.

20. Robert L. Katz, "Jewish Values and Sociopsychological Perspectives on Aging," *Pastoral Psychology* 24, 229 (winter 1975), 148.

21. Reich, *The Future of Success*, 217.

22. Richard W. Judy and Carol D'Amico, *Workforce 2020* (Indianapolis: Hudson Institute, 1998), 94.

23. Richard W. Judy, "The Cumming Retirement Torrent," *American Outlook*, fall 1998, 28–31.

24. Dave Patel, "Rearranging the Life Cycle," *HR Magazine*, January 2002, 104. Reprinted with the permission of *HR Magazine*, published by the Society for Human Resource Management, Alexandria, VA.

25. Ken Dychtwald, *Age Wave* (New York: Bantam Books, 1990), 30, 31.

26. Deloss L. Marsh, *Retirement Careers* (Charlotte, Vermont: Williamson Publishing, 1991), 13–23.

27. Sheehy, *Understanding Men's Passages*, 240.

28. Katz, "Jewish Values and Sociopsychological Perspectives on Aging," 136.

29. Ibid., 149.

30. Lou Ann Walker, "We Can Control How We Age," *Parade Magazine*, September 16, 2001, 4, 5.

31. Katz, "Jewish Values and Sociopsychological Perspectives on Aging," 141.

Epilogue

1. Stephen Franklin, "The Too-Fast Track," *Chicago Tribune*, January 28, 2001, Book Section, 3.

2. Steven Greenhouse, "In U.S., Workers Toil Even Longer," *Chicago Tribune*, September 1, 2001, Section 1, 1, 10.

3. Mary Schmich, "Good Work Often Unnoticed—No Thanks to Most," *Chicago Tribune*, September 2, 2001, Metro Section, 1.

4. Fred Moody, "When Work Becomes an Obsession," *Utne Reader*, July–August 1988, 65.

5. A Private Conversation, "Meeting for the Society of Business Ethics," Washington D.C., August 14, 15, 16, 2001.

6. Wayne Muller, *Sabbath* (New York: Bantam Books, 1999), 176.

7. Daniel J. Boorstin, *The Image* (New York: Atheneum, 1980), 4.

8. Muller, *Sabbath*, 100.

9. Richard L. Lippke, "Five Concerns Regarding the Commercialization of Leisure," *Business and Society Review* 106, 2 (summer 2001), 125.

10. Ibid., 110–120.

11. Anthony Storr, *Solitude* (New York: Ballantine Books, 1989), 16–41.

12. Muller, *Sabbath*, 1, 88.

13. Ibid., 8.

14. Ibid., 10.

15. Ibid., 19.

16. Ibid., 212.

17. Bradley K. Googins, *Work/Family Conflicts* (Wesport, Conn.: Auburn House, 1991), 3, 4, 5.

18. Tenay A. Darlington, "Slow Is Beautiful," *Utne Reader*, November–December 2000, 55; Also see www.mcdonalds.com.

19. Ibid., 55, 56, 57.

20. Leon R. Kass, *The Hungry Soul* (Chicago: University of Chicago Press, 1999), 10.

21. "Breaking Point," *Newsweek*, November 6, 1995, 56–62.

22. Arlie Russell Hochschild, *The Second Shift* (New York: Viking, 1989), 9.

23. "Breaking Point," 58.

24. "Sleepy on the Job? You're Not Alone," *Chicago Sun-Times*, March 28, 2001, Section 1, 1, 29.

25. Ronald Kotulak, "Waking Up to Danger of Sleep Deprivation," *Chicago Tribune*, May 27, 2001, Section 1, 1, 14.

About the Author

Al Gini is Professor of Philosophy at Loyola University, Chicago. He is also the co-founder and Associate Editor of *Business Ethics Quarterly*, the journal of the Society for Business Ethics. Besides lecturing to community and professional organizations, he does consulting on corporate ethics and employee relations and can be regularly heard on *National Public Radio*'s Chicago affiliate, WBEZ-FM. His published works include, *It Comes with the Territory: An Inquiry into the Nature of Work* (with T. Sullivan) and *Case Studies in Business Ethics* (with Thomas Donaldson). He has also written and produced a play, *Working Ourselves to Death*. His most recent book is entitled, *My Job My Self: Work and the Creation of the Modern Individual*, published by Routledge.

Index